A Fresh Look

at the

Dokdo

Issue

Japanese Scholars Review Historical Facts

Translated by M. Marek and S. J. Choi

DADAMEDIA

A Fresh Look at the Dokdo Issue:
Japanese Scholars Review Historical Facts

First published in 2006
© 2006 by S. J. Choi

Translated by M. Marek and S. J. Choi
Book design & layout by **DADAMEDIA**
Edited by **DADAMEDIA**
Published in 2006 by **DADAMEDIA** Total Publications & Circulations

Suite 502, Chungmu Bldg, 70−20 Yekwan−Dong Chung−Gu,
Seoul, Korea, 100−290.
Publisher: Boo−Nam Lee
Phone: 82−(0)2−2277−7667
Fax: 82−(0)2−2268−8052
E−mail: dada@dadamedia.co.kr
Find us on the World Wide Web at www.dadamedia.co.kr

ISBN: 89−7114−078−X

A Fresh Look
at the Dokdo Issue:

Japanese Scholars Review Historical Facts

Dokdo is the name of the island situated approximately midway between Korea and Japan, in the East Sea. Surrounded by a cluster of 89 rocks, it comprises two large islands, Dongdo (East Island) and Seodo(West Island). The area of Dongdo is 73,297m², and Seodo has an area of 88,639m². The total land area of Dokdo is 187,453m².

Though Dokdo was a lonely island for centuries, home to only seabirds and seals, that is no longer the case. Dokdo has residents who live on it all year round. At the moment, 37 Korean police officers, three lighthouse keepers and a Korean fisherman and his wife are residents of Dokdo. There are also four ferries operated by two Korean companies that shuttle regularly between Ulleungdo, its closest neighbor, and Dokdo. These ferries have delivered thousands of Korean tourists to Dokdo since the launch of the tour service in 2005.

Dokdo may not be a large island, but it deserves far greater attention than its physical size would imply. Dokdo matters a great deal in Korea–Japan relations, as it has constituted one of the most enduring sources of misunderstanding between the two Asian neighbors. The Japanese government has infuriated Koreans by challenging the well–established conviction that Dokdo is Korean.

Not only has Dokdo mattered in the area of international relations and diplomacy, but it has also constituted an important item of academic controversy between Korean and Japanese scholars. Since at least the 1950s, a large volume of academic work has been published in the two countries on the Dokdo issue. Yet despite the unquestion -able academic interest in Dokdo, even a basic review of the literature reveals that Japan's *raison d'etre* in many instances has been to support established national positions. Here we are reminded of the points raised by Victor Prescott in his classic work on the geography of inter -national boundaries, quoting Siegfried when noting the propensity of the promotion of national interest to flavor the outcome of research:

"The study of boundaries is dangerous...because it is also thoroughly charged with political passions and entirely encumbered with afterthoughts. The people are too interested in the issue when they speak of boundaries to speak with detachment: the failing is permanent."

Yet there has been notable exception to this well-established pattern, specifically Japanese scholars Matsumoto Takeo(松本健男), Ikeuchi Satoshi(池內敏) and Naitō Seichū(內藤正中). Their articles are actually more supportive of Korean claims and offer up the view that Japanese conduct toward Dokdo has been, for the most part, a by-product of its imperialist past.

The icy tension between Korea and Japan surrounding Dokdo can probably be assuaged by diplomatic negotiations and political compromises, but an ultimate solution to this emotional issue can only be achieved through the rightful interpretation of historical facts. In this respect, the Dokdo conundrum is more of an historical issue than it is about international law and politics. It is no exaggeration to say that it constitutes one integral part of Northeast Asian history controversies centered around key Japanese figures' visits to the *Yasukuni* shrine, Japanese school history textbooks and the interpretation of the Nanking massacre.

This book has compiled four articles written by three Japanese scholars. Their work is unique in that their views make a departure from the majority of Japanese voices devoted to bolstering the country's claims. The original text of these articles was written in Japanese. This simple fact has limited the chance for non−Japanese speakers to take advantage of these scholars' fresh look at the Dokdo issue. The aim in publishing this book is to bring those non−Japanese speakers widened access to such nonpartisan voices from Japan's academic circle.

Contents

How to Achieve a Fair Solution to the Senkaku Islands and Takeshima Problems

Recognizing the Need to View the Issue as a Result of Policies of Aggression

Matsumoto Takeo(松本健男)

(1)

The 1996 Japanese—American Joint Security Declaration lifted the restrictions of the 1960 Security Treaty and ushered in an era of even tighter cooperation in the area of defense concerning geographical scope and contents. We now understand that from this point on momentous change would be demanded of our nation's (Japan's) political structure.

The scope of declaration includes the launch of a study on Japanese–US cooperation regarding situations that may arise within Japan's vicinity, affecting the peace and security of Japan and on unresolved territorial disputes as sources of insecurity within the Asia–Pacific region. The following statement was made as part of the declaration.

"The two leaders... emphasised that it is extremely important for the stability and prosperity of the region that China play a positive and constructive role, and, in this context, stressed the interest of both countries in furthering cooperation with China." This short quote reflects how Japan and the US, the two predominant allies in the Asia–Pacific region, are concerned about China's increasing influence within the area amid attempts to solidify their predominance over the Asia–Pacific region.

The debate on the ownership of the Senkaku Islands, which had been on the back burner until now reignited as this new political situation unfolded. At the same time questions about the sovereignty of Takeshima(The Japanese call Dokdo Takeshima) reappeared on the agenda with Korea. In spite of Chinese and Korean ownership, the Japanese government still considers these islands indigenous Japanese territory. This paper investigates whether this standpoint is justified and suggests a point of view that Japanese citizens should consider.

(2)

It can now be understood that a statement issued on March 3, 1972 by the Ministry of Foreign Affairs of Japan(MOFA) may constitute the official Japanese government's view in claiming Japanese sovereignty over the Senkaku Islands.

According to this, in 1895 the Meiji government repeatedly surveyed the Senkaku Islands through local Okinawa Prefecture. After finding them uninhabited and after carefully checking for any signs of Ching China's control, the Meiji government formally incorporated the Senkaku Islands into Japanese national territory on January 1, 1895 through a cabinet decision to put up a national mark on them. This group of islands is part of Nanseishotō(南西諸島), which is also our (Japan's) indigenous territory. However, they are not included in article 2 of the 1895 Treaty of Shimonoseki which required that China cede Taiwan and the Penghu Islands to Japan. So is Japan's indigenous territory rationale indeed legitimate?

In 1972, Kyoto University Professor Inoue Kiyoshi(井上 清)'s articles concluded that the Senkaku Islands belonged to China. In his article "Imperial Expansionism" carried in volume 16 of Habōhō Kenkyū(坡防法研究)[The Study on the Subversive Activities Prevention Act], Inoue writes that in the late Ming Dynasty a delegation sailing from Fuzhou(福州) to Naha(那覇), the capital of Okinawa, mentions sailing past the Uotsurishima(釣魚島), Kōbishima(黃尾嶼) and Sekioshima(赤尾嶼) before reaching Kumeshima(久米島), one of the Okinawan Islands, in their log book.

The oldest records of the Okinawan Kingdom are the Ryūkyūkoku Chūzan Seikan(琉球國中山世鑑) written in 1650 by the Okinawan consul. The text quotes the Ming delegation's log using the exact same words. The text Chūsan Denshinroku(中山傳信錄) published after the Ching Dynasty by an official envoy, mentions Okinawa as an island situated in the waters bordering on China and the Ryukyus. A Japanese text Sankoku Tsūran Zusetsu(三國通覽圖說), published before the Meiji reform took place, also mentions the Senkaku Islands. The author Hayashi Shihei was an administrator in late Edo period(from 1783−93) and also an intellectual who devoted himself to the philosophy of relieving people's suffering. The text includes a map depicting the Senkaku Islands with the same color cherry blossoms as its Chinese motherland. Based on these historical facts, it is proven that the Senkaku Islands were originally Chinese territory distinct from Okinawa.

Inoue refers to various important points explaining how Japan incorporated the islands. For example, in 1885, businessman Koga Tatsushiro(古賀辰四郎) appealed to Okinawa Prefecture for a loan of land to help establish a new business venture. Home Affairs Minister Yamakata Aritomo(山縣有朋) took the opportunity and ordered a survey of the uninhabited islands scattered between Okinawa Prefecture and Ching China's Fuzhou. Okinawa Prefecture submitted a report to Yamakata in September of the same year. It stated that the Senkaku Islands described in Chūsan Denshinroku may actually be the Uotsuridai(釣魚臺). Anxious to plant a national mark on the 'newly discovered land', they suggested another urgent survey. The report also states that they were also awaiting further instructions from the ministry. Home Affairs Minister Yamakata wrote to the Minister for Foreign Affairs Inoue Kaoru(井上馨) who replied that

Japan was on China's side these days, and that there were already rumours circulating about the Japanese government occupying islands within China's territory. Inoue Kaoru also wrote that planting any national mark on new territory was futile, as it would only arouse Chinese suspicion. He ended his communique by hinting that dispatching an expedition party to survey the islands should be all for now on the matter. In December of the same year the home affairs and foreign ministers issued jointly signed instructions reminding Okinawa Prefecture that it was not immediately necessary to publicly stamp the islands Japanese yet.

After that in 1890 and 1893, the Okinawan governor wrote to the government stating he would like to bring the Senkaku Islands and the other islets under Japanese jurisdiction. The ministries did not reply or grant him any consent.

The Japanese government decided to incorporate the Senkaku Islands into Japanese territory in 1894. This had become possible after the surprise Japanese attack and declaration of war with China in July 1894. In December Japan became sure that it would win the war, and on January 14, 1895 the Cabinet decided to incorporate the islands and display a Japanese mark on them.

These events are historical facts and Professor Inoue published the original documents providing a detailed review. There is absolutely no reason to refute these facts. Therefore MOFA's original claims that Ching China was not in control of the islands was a seriously misleading statement to make.

According to MOFA, the Senkaku Islands were not part of the territories ceded to Japan as a result of the Treaty of Shimonoseki(下關條約); that they had rather been acquired 'naturally'. Therefore the islands were indigenous national territory and there was no need to return them to China. Can such data supply acceptable details to conclude the issue once and for all?

(3)

The Senkaku Islands are scattered over an area of about 100km² to the south of the Ryukyu Islands and about 180km north of Ishigakishima(石垣島). They are on the easternmost edge of the Chinese continental shelf. A 2200m deep oceanic trough runs between the Senkaku and Ryukyu Islands, and the Kuroshio Current(黑潮) flows northwards dividing the two territories. Taiwanese fishermen operate in that area. For us living in Japan it would be easy to say that Senkaku belongs to Okinawa, but the distance between the Senkaku Islands and Ryukyu Islands is further than from Tokyo to Shizuoka(靜岡), or Osaka(大阪) to Okayama(岡山). Geographically they do not form part of the Ryukyus. As mentioned above the Senkaku Islands are located on the shipping route from Fujian Province of China to Okinawa; and the distance between Sekiosho(赤尾嶼), the easternmost island of the Senkaku Islands, and the western edge of Kumeshima(久米島) to the west of Okinawa is just 220km. Thus there is no proof that Japanese citizens knew that the Senkaku Islands existed in the old days, or of their interest in them at all. But they attempted to incorporate the islands as part of the new Meiji government's nationalist policy of expansionism taking advantage of Koga Tatsushiro's communique. The government's actions before 1895 appear exceedingly cautious. Reason for this wariness was the fact that Japan had indeed ascertained that the islands in question were within Chinese territory and was afraid of being entangled in a fracas should Japanese interest in the islets become too obvious.

Japan had achieved full military success over Ching China in the war. However up until then they had not at all been confident they could win a full on military confrontation with China, despite the fact that the Ching dynasty was in decline. This was the major reason why the Japanese government had been reluctant about seizing the Senkaku Islands earlier. When China ceded Taiwan, Japan occupied the 'affiliated' Senkaku Islands, thus in their opinion concluding the issue of jurisdiction altogether. Looking at these circumstances objectively, the means by which the aggressor, Japan, acquired Taiwan and the Penghu Islands (through war) and the seizure of the Senkaku Islands are fundamentally the same.

Under the terms of surrender, Japan had accepted the Potsdam Declaration that stipulates that Japan shall fulfil the terms of the Cairo Declaration. The Cairo Declaration stipulates that "all the territories Japan has stolen from the Chinese, such as Manchuria, Formosa, and the Pescadores, shall be restored to the Republic of China." Mentioned before, the Japanese MOFA does not consider the Senkaku Islands part of the territories ceded by China(such as Taiwan and Penghu) in article 2 of the Treaty of Shimonoseki. How can one say that the islands were not taken from China in the same fashion as were Taiwan, Penghu and Manchuria? China was forced to hand over Taiwan and the Penghu Islands, and Japan implemented its decision to take the Senkaku Islands at virtually the same time in January and April 1895. All this was part of the Sino–Japanese War. Considering this, we must conclude that by not returning the Senkaku Islands, Japan is not fulfilling its duties accepted in the Potsdam Declaration. Japan's claim to the Senkaku Islands is definitely not sanctioned by international law.

(4)

The following section sheds light on the issue of Takeshima. Takeshima or Dokdo(in Korean) is situated 49 nautical miles east–south–east of Ulleungdo in the Sea of Japan. It is a group of rocks that fits in an area 400m by 400m, with a summit 174m above sea level. Just as the Senkaku Islands, it is unable to support human life and thus has been uninhabited. However, on January 28, 1905 Japan reached a cabinet decision calling it Takeshima. Following this official act, the governor of Shimane Prefecture incorporated Takeshima into Japanese territory by issuing 'Public Notice No. 40' stating "from now on, the islands' jurisdiction lies with the governor of Oki Island," and the Japanese takeover was completed. This was a time of many historical events, the declaration of war with Russia in February 1904 and the forced signing of the Japanese–Korean protocol, effectively bringing the whole of Korea under Japanese rule, while also launching its military occupation. The August 1905 peace treaty, concluded as a result of the Japanese victory, obligated Russia to approve Japanese predominance over Korea in the areas of politics, economics, and the military. In November 1905, without any prior debate, Japan highhandedly demanded that the Korean Emperor sign a pact amounting to total submission as a colony. The Korean Righteous Army forces tried to resist, but the uprising was thoroughly suppressed and they were absorbed into the Japanese army when the annexation was completed in 1910. The Korean government and people had absolutely no latitude at that time to protest against the takeover of Takeshima.

So, how come Korea and Japan both thought Takeshima originally belonged to them? There appear to be opposing standpoints. Without going into detail, since the island is affiliated with Ulleungdo, one comes to the simple conclusion that Korea holds the rights to the territory. Mainly fishermen from Ulleungdo fish the surrounding waters. It is widely known that when Japanese fishing boats sail from Izumo(出雲) to fish around Ulleungdo, they follow a sea route overlooking Takeshima(Dokdo). Interestingly from 1430 onward a Korean law had banned its citizens from sailing to or fishing near the island for 300 years. Of course Japanese fishermen from Izumo were not subject to such a law and fished Ulleungdo's rich waters. However, in 1881 the Korean government changed its policy and even encouraged settlers to move there. On October 27, 1900, the Korean government issued 'Imperial Ordinance No. 41' that appointed a governor for the whole of Ulleungdo and Dokdo. (Quoted from Kajimura Hideki[梶村秀樹]: 「The Takeshima=Dokdo issue and the Japanese State」 in Chōsen Kenkyū(朝鮮研究) [Korean Studies] September 1978). Such historical facts show that Shimane Prefecture's style of proclaiming the island Japanese territory was clearly illegal, as Takeshima was already linked with the Korean state.

So, how did the issue develop when Japan surrendered after World War Two?

On January 29, 1946 the Supreme Commander for the Allied Powers issued a memorandum on governmental and administrative separation of certain outlying areas from Japan. Among the territories considered separated from Japan were Ulleungdo, Takeshima and Jejudo. This note would suggest that the Allied Powers considered Takeshima, just as Ulleungdo and Jejudo, as territory belonging to Korea. The San Francisco Peace Treaty, signed in September 1951, ruled that, "Japan, recognizing the independence of Korea, renounces all right, title and claim to Korea, including the islands of Quelpart (Jejudo), Port Hamilton (Geomundo) and Dagelet (Ulleungdo)." Still Japan does not accept the return of Takeshima as one of the conditions stipulated in this treaty. Many Japanese still believe that Takeshima belongs to Japan, since the peace treaty omitted Takeshima in those areas to be separated from Japan. However, in considering the examples of Jejudo, Geomundo and Ulleungdo, it seems very possible that Takeshima as an island affiliated with Ulleungdo, therefore, actually is part of Ulleungdo. So, using the San Francisco treaty as evidence that Takeshima is Japanese territory is wrong.

After Japan's defeat, Korea was liberated, and looking to establish its control, set up fishing grounds around Ulleungdo. In August 1949[sic] the newly formed Korean government finalized formal proceedings to exercise their authority over the island. In 1952 Japan and Korea entered a serious dispute over Takeshima/Dokdo ownership when Korea issued a "Presidential Proclamation of Sovereignty over the Adjacent Seas" and established the 'Rhee Syngman Line' including the waters around Dokdo. As a result Japan started a vicious campaign focusing on Takeshima. In May 1954 Japanese fishermen from Oki Islands landed on the island and started collecting[mussels, sea kelp etc.] in broad daylight. However, the Korean National Assembly, passed a "resolution to protect Dokdo from Japanese Invasion" and the Korean government built a lighthouse and stationed a permanent guards there in August 1954. In 1996 work began on a bulwark and a pier.

(5)

The events described above hint at the essence of Japanese expansionism. One can say that both the Senkaku Islands and Takeshima have distinct 'characters' and must be placed with either China or Korea respectively. Furthermore, one should realize that Japan's claims are illegal under international law, because they are linked to events surrounding the invasions. There is a complete lack of any true basis to what the Japanese government emphasizes are rightful claims to 'indigenous territory'.

Political parties of Japan, such as the Liberal Democratic Party, Progressive Party and even the Communist Party share this view, denouncing China, South Korea and North Korea who assert their inherent rights. Such Japanese political parties' behaviour is unforgivable. On September 22, 1996 Akahata(赤旗: an organ of the Japan Communist Party) ran a feature article about the Senkaku Issue. The article read: "Japanese measures to take over the islands in 1895 were the first act of laying claim to the Senkaku Islands. The acquisition took place in conformity with international law and was based on a history of occupation and effective rule." Since 1972 the Japanese Communist Party has consistently emphasized that the Senkaku Islands is clearly Japanese indigenous territory. If we look closely at international law on the subject, it says that occupation in accordance with international law can be established if a state occupies *terra nullius*(no man's land). The principles supporting this illogical law served as a means of supporting the imperialist powers' bid to carve up the world into colonies. Its interpretation makes it legal to take over even inhabited territories because the inhabitants were mere 'savages' who had not formed a recognizable state. (Yokoda Kisaburō[横田喜三郎], Kokusaihō II [國際法II], Hōrizugaku Zenshu[法律學全集], Yuhikaku[有斐閣], published in 1972.) This amounted to what was no more than legalized robbery completely disregarding the rights of indigenous residents. The Senkaku Islands and Takeshima are lonely islands in the distant sea where people could not live. The waters around these islands represented the livelihood of local fishermen(living on Ulleungdo). No such circumstances had been established whereupon Japan could assume effective control of them. Japan seized the land when China and Korea were under military oppression. In order to justify their move, Japan fabricated claims about China and Korea not exercising any authority over the islands.

In order to justify taking over vast areas of land, the Japanese government pursues the 'indigenous territory theory', and some scholars of international law and the Japanese Communist Party refer to 'sovereignty acquired through occupation'. However, these theories were devised in order to hide years of endless cruelty suffered by the local Chinese and Korean peoples throughout the 19th century. In doing so, the Japanese government and people are denying themselves their true part within the international community.

Still, the Japanese government must retract their claims to the Senkaku Islands and Takeshima, and acknowledge Chinese and Korean territorial sovereignty over these islands, seeking a way to develop the waters jointly. These prerequisites would lead to good neighbourly relations and bring great benefits for our nation(Japan).

In order to resolve the island disputes, Japan must change its policy, which has remained much the same since the end of the war 50 years ago. Furthermore, Japan needs to address the continuing icy nationalistic sentiment alive in Japanese society today. To overcome all these problems, Japan just needs to free itself from all the old shameful relics dating back to its invasion of Asia.

[Original 『社會評論』 Vol. 23 No. 2, pp.32-38]

Is Takeshima(竹島) Japanese indigenous Territory?

Naitō Seichū(內藤正中)[1]

1. The stir created by the designation of 'Takeshima Day'

With the climax of the 'Korean Wave', this year was called the 'Year of Japanese–Korean Friendship'. Consequently both sides were expecting great progress in friendly relations between the two countries, Japan and Korea. However, Shimane Prefecture Council incurred a strong rebuke from

---

1) Professor Emeritus Shimane University, former Head of the North East Asia Research Institute at Tottori Womens' University Junior College and visiting professor.

Korea by passing a bill establishing 'Takeshima Day'. In addition, a huge stir is spreading with various cooperating business ventures taking place on either side, being suspended.

Takeshima is an island belonging to Oki(隱岐), Shimamachi (島町) in Shimane Prefecture. However, in Korea this island is called Dokdo and belongs to Ulleung−eup(Ulleung town) in Gyeongsangbuk−do Province, and the on−going dispute over the island's jurisdiction dates back to former times.

In 1951, the Shimane Prefecture side submitted a petition with the title 'Reconfirming Takeshima as Shimane Prefecture Territory' and has continued to submit a copy whenever any-thing happens. This is why the prefecture(縣) dared to take decisive action and establish a regulation by itself in order to incite the Japanese government, which had not assumed any role in the matter.

Takeshima appeared on the map of Shimane Prefecture only recently. Likewise, the people living in the prefecture show little interest in the matter. Not knowing when, but acknowledging that the situation would spark a row Gyeongsangbuk−do Province and Shimane Prefecture, both of which have administrative jurisdiction over Dokdo, established sisterhood relations, and 15 years have passed since. Naturally, one would assume that some progress had been made on research into Takeshima. However, only a few studies have touched upon the subject. The present situation is the result of avoiding confrontation with the past, and the attitude that the problem of territorial jurisdiction is only a matter for the government.

In other words, the dispute over Takeshima stands at the forefront of the territorial dispute. Shimane Prefecture never expected that it would provoke Korea to such an extent. This shows the differences in their understanding of history. I think that if one wishes to take action, one must do so after having studied the situation completely. For instance, when looking at the Shimane Prefecture public broadcast shown on a commercial TV station, or the intent behind the Prefecture Council's institution of the bill, one finds that they are no more than a copy of the Ministry of Foreign Affairs'(MOFA) misconception.

I am in doubt of MOFA's standpoint claiming that "historically and under international law, (Dokdo) is Japanese territory". Therefore, in this paper I will investigate whether this really is the case.

2. Seafaring Enterprise to Takeshima(竹島渡海) during the Edo(江戸) Period

MOFA's internet homepage describes the following passages under the title 'The Historical Truth about the Ownership of Takeshima'.

> In the early Edo period(1618), after receiving(拝領 [*hairyō*]) Ulleungdo from the *Shogunate* the two houses of Ooya(大谷) and Murakawa(村川) of Hokihan(伯耆 藩) acquired the right to sail there. Every year, they went to this island to fish, and presented Abalone to the *Shogunate*. At that time, Takeshima was being used as a port of call on the way to Ulleungdo and as a fishing area. [Also], at least in 1661, they received(拝領) Takeshima as well.

Based on this historical description, MOFA claims that "at the latest, by the mid−17th century, our country had established sovereignty over Takeshima by effective occupation." Is such a conclusion really possible?

First, there never existed a *Han*(藩) by the name of 'Hokishū'. It was common practice to use the names Tottorihan or Inshūhan because these *Han*[a prefecture] had Inaba and Hoki under their jurisdiction, and had a castle in Tottori. It would be deplorable to think the name could have been influenced by Korea calling it Hokishū (伯耆州).

Next, it says that they received(拝領) the authority to govern Ulleungdo and Takeshima from the *Shogunate*. However, this is absolutely untrue. Here, what MOFA calls Takeshima was called Matsushima(松島) at that time, which is today's Takeshima. I shall use 竹島(Ulleungdo) and 松島(present−day Takeshima) respectively in accordance with previous instances. The fact that the Ooya family received the authority to govern the island from the *chogunate* can be found in the Ooya family(大谷家) records. These were borrowed from a document with the title 'A Duplicate of an Extracted Account of Sailing to Takeshima' made in 1810 by the 11th *Tōshu*(当主)[a present master]. The documents of the Ooya family were almost entirely lost to a fire, and the 'Duplicate of an Extracted Account' is a collection of the remaining documents. The word *Hairyō*(拝領)[receive] appears in a 請書 (a document replying to questions and orders from the 巡見使) sent to the *Junkenshi*(巡見使)[an official who inspects a state instead of the *Shogun*] by *Tōshu* in 1681.

Since in a feudal society all land is owned by the feudal lord, it is impossible that the *chogunate* distributed (分封) islands to its *Chōnin*(町人) [people living around the castle, namely townspeople].

Thirdly, Kawakami Kenzō(川上健三) says that the *chogunate* only permitted 渡海(crossing the sea) to 竹島 (Ulleungdo). Concerning sea crossings to 松島(present−day Takeshima) they "merely obtained the *Shogunate's Naii*(內意)[private opinion] on the matter"(*Takeshima no Rekishi Chirigakudeki Kenkyu*[竹島の 歷史地理學的 研究]A Study of Takeshima from a Standpoint of Historical Geography,1966). Kawakami was a researcher for the Treaty Bureau of MOFA and was working on making it clear that Takeshima was historically Japanese territory.

If, as MOFA claims, the *chogunate* gave Ulleungdo to the people, then this would have meant that Ulleungdo was Japanese territory and there would have been no need to issue a special permit for crossing the sea. The reason why the Lord of Tottori applied for the permit from the *Shogunate* and the *Shogunate* granted it, was that there were concerns that Ulleungdo may have been Korean territory. Tsushimahan(大馬藩)had been plotting to take possession of Ulleungdo calling it Isotakeshima(磯竹島) just before the

Tottori received the permit for it in 1614. At that time, Korea protested strongly and sent a statement saying that the sea route for coming−and−going to Korea was only through Tsushima, and that those visiting Korea's shores by any other root would be considered pirates. Thus, the *chogunate* was not able to issue the Yonago(米子) people, who wanted to sail to Takeshima(Ulleungdo), with a *Shuinjō*(朱印狀) permitting to trade overseas. Instead, the only form of authorization they could give was a *Hōshō*(奉書)[an official letter].

A *Hōshō* is a document, jointly signed by the *Rōjū*(老中)[the highest level among warrior officials, about three people], allowing only the holder himself to sail abroad. It is a rare case indeed that the receiver of a seafaring permit, in this case to Takeshima, was a lord of *Han* himself. Moreover, the *chogunate* issued a certificate called *Kondotokai*(今度渡海), which sanctioned crossing the sea no more than once. Accordingly, they should have had to re−apply to the government every time they wanted to cross the sea (to Ulleungdo). However, referring to this, Kawakami Kenzō wondered whether the *chogunate* may have treated Takeshima(Ulleungdo) as Japanese territory, and thus, considered traveling there 'movement within' the nation's borders.

Further, there is the problem of whether one can believe the issue date 1618 to be correct. The Ooya family abstract states that the crossings started in 1618. This is the prevalent view and the foreign ministry also states this. Yet, the document merely shows 'May 16' with no sign of the year referred to. Besides, among the four signatories were only two *Rōjū*, and the remaining two signatories were *Koshōkumibantō*(小姓組番頭)[subordinate to the *Rōjū*].

All four were appointed *Rōjū* in 1622. Thus, the document must obviously have been issued later than 1618.

It is peculiar that MOFA concludes that the year 1661 is connected to the award of present−day Takeshima, then called Matsushima. The year 1661 was used because Kawakami said that "1661 was the year the Ooya and Murakawa families became able to sail to present−day Takeshima with formal recognition of the *Shogunate*". Several years in which sea crossings took place appear in the Ooya family document. However, this means no more than that they were able to sail to Matsushima(present−day Takeshima). Kawakami also could not record more than "gaining the *Shogunate's Naii*(內意)[private opinion]". Thus, one cannot take this and claim that "in 1661 the *Shogunate* awarded both families".

3. The Ban on Sailing to Takeshima(Ulleungdo) and Matsushima(present-day Takeshima)

The people of Yonago(米子) had engaged in seafaring enterprise on and around Takeshima(Ulleungdo) for 70 years from the first half of the 17th century. They brought back precious goods such as abalone, seal oil, paulownia wood and medicinal herbs. It is written that the people "do not pay tributes in kind" to the *chogunate*. However, they gave skewered abalone to prominent figures in the *chogunate*, or sent paulownia wood to anyone who wanted it. In addition, Tottorihan loaned a thousand sacks of rice every year as expenses for the seafaring, gave support by lending the lord of a *Han* money, or settled accounts by exchanging skewered abalone for money.

This is how Takeshima(Ulleungdo) became known as an island belonging to the Hoki state, and Saito Hōsen wrote in 1667 that Matsushima were in the northwest of the Oki State. This historical document received attention because it is the first written record of Matsushima(present-day Takeshima). Yet, both countries(Japan and Korea) conflict over whether one should consider Takeshima(Ulleungdo) or Oki the north-western border of Japan. I think that because sea crossings to Takeshima(Ulleungdo) were at their most frequent at the time, the people of Oki recognized the island as Japanese territory belonging to the Hoki State. Had this not been the case, then a territorial dispute, the case concerning Takeshima(竹島一件), between Japan and Korea 30 years later would have been without cause.

The 'case concerning Takeshima' concluded with the confirmation that Takeshima(Ulleungdo) was Korean territory. Saying settlers would attract raids by Japanese pirates, the Korean government introduced a policy banning people from settling on the island after the 15th century. Needless to say, this does not mean they gave up sovereignty over the island. However, the people of Yonago(米子) were able to carry on sailing to the island, because it was uninhabited. Yet, this behaviour is merely on a par with breaking into a house while the owner is away and stealing valuable goods. One cannot claim that such theft is equivalent to what the Ministry of Foreign Affairs writes on its internet homepage: "Based upon effective control over the island, our country established sovereignty over Takeshima by the mid−17th century at the latest".

In 1693, Korea protested about people from Yonago sailing to Takeshima. That year people from Yonago sailed to Takeshima and saw that there were already Koreans living there. They reported this to the *Han* office and handed in a Korean hat and woven headband as evidence. Tottorihan demanded that the *Shogunate* deal with this problem.

In the following year again Korean people were on the island already [before the Japanese]. Two of the Koreans were taken to Yonago and were detained for two months. They were sent to Nagasaki, then were sent home via Tsushimahan on orders of the *Shogunate*. At that time, the *chogunate* ordered Tsushimahan to request that Korea forbid its people from coming to Takeshima.

In response, Korea asserted that the "Takeshima the Japanese talk about is our Ulleungdo". The ensuing diplomatic negotiations called the 'case concerning Takeshima' lasted for three years. The result was that the *chogunate* prohibited seafaring to Takeshima and notified Tottorihan of this.

Further to this, MOFA's homepage claims that, "Sailing to Ulleungdo was forbidden, yet, sailing to Takeshima was not". Thus, it is saying that there was no mention of a ban on landing at Takeshima(Matsushima).

However, since Matsushima is an island associated with Takeshima, it was not given any special attention. Thus, a separate seafaring license was not even issued, and there was no need to refer to it separately. Since Matsushima was an island that ships just passed by or briefly anchored at on their way to Takeshima(Ulleungdo), no one sailed out merely for the purpose of landing on Matsushima when sailing to Takeshima(Ulleungdo) was forbidden.

In either case, the important point is that the *Shogunate* was forced to ban sailing to Takeshima in response to a document presented to the *Shogunate* by Tottorihan on December 25, 1695.

Abebunggokami(阿部豊後守), a *Rōjū* to Tottorihan, had put forward seven questions raised by Tottorihan regarding Takeshima on December 24. The first of the questions raised was: "When was Takeshima included into Inshū(因州) and Hokishū(伯州)?". Tottorihan replied, "Takeshima does not belong to Inshū and Hokishū." And, replying to the seventh question, "Are there any other islands the two nations(Inshū and Hokishū) have jurisdiction over apart from Takeshima?", the *chogunate* replied: "There are no islands the two nations have jurisdiction over, including Takeshima and Matsushima". Important here is that Tottorihan stated that "both nations

Inshū(因州) and Hakushū(伯州) did not include" Takeshima and Matsushima (present−day Takeshima). One cannot say that islands, not belonging to Inshū or Hakushū, were Japanese territory. In other words, one cannot say that where sailing to Takeshima was prohibited, the ban would not apply to Matsushima.

As long as Ulleungdo, then called Takeshima, was considered Korean, then Matsushima(present−day Takeshima), Ulleungdo's sister island, is also Korean.

4. Ahn Yong−bok's protest visit to Tottori

The Japanese side knew that Matsushima existed along the route to Takeshima. Although the Korean side has a record describing the Usan state of Ulleungdo being merged with Silla in 512, there is no entry mentioning Dokdo. The existence of another island different from Ulleungdo became known in the mid−15th century. The *Uljinhyeon Jo* [Article on Uljin County] in the *Sejong Sillok Jiriji*(世宗實 錄地理志)[Geographical Appendix to the Annals of King Sejong] describes that, "Two islands, Usan and Mureung, are located in the sea to the east of Uljin County, and the two islands are not far apart. When it is clear and bright due to wind, one can see from one to the other". However, because there was a ban on settling on Ulleungdo, this report would merely have been written by a civil servant who was sent there occasionally. There is no information collected from local people, and no one tried to confirm the actual existence of Usando.

Hence, for example, the map of Gangwon Province appearing in *Sinjeung Dongguk Yeoji Seungnam*(新增東國輿地勝覽)[Revised and Augmented Version of the Survey of the National Geography of Korea], published in 1521, depicted Usando to the west and of the same size as Ulleungdo. It is said that the island was initially called Usando, then appeared with names such as Sambongdo and Gajido. Yet, one cannot conclude that it is present−day Dokdo. However, because in 1696 Ahn Yong−bok from Dongrae came to Japan to protest before Tottorihan that Usando was different from Ulleungdo, one must conclude that information about the island was already wide spread.

Ahn's visit to Japan receives special mention in Korean middle and high school history textbooks for asserting before the *Shogunate* that Dokdo was under Korean jurisdiction. Yet, in Japan this historical event is considered a nonsensical statement made by an impersonator or an individual prone to exaggeration (etc.). Despite being an important diplomatic issue, they ignored Ahn's visit. Consequently, it does not even appear in *Tottorikenshi*(鳥取縣史)[History of Tottori Prefecture].

On the Korean side there are historical records relating to this incident for example *Joseon Wangjo Sillok*. It records how Ahn Yong−bok was arrested by the *Bibyeonsa* (備邊司)[Border Defense Command] and interrogated after returning from Japan. That is to say, Ahn Yong−bok saw Japanese people on Ulleungdo and chased them to Usando saying, "As Matsushima is Jasando it thus belongs to us." Jasando is Usando. Yet, in January of that year, the ban on sailing to Takeshima was enforced and the people of Yonago did not go to the island anymore. Therefore, Ahn Yong−bok's remarks and actions are made into nothing but lies.

There is a historical document held by Tottorihan, which describes Ahn Young−bok's arrival and two months stay in the Hoki state in detail. I have previously mentioned this in 竹島(鬱陵島)を めぐる 日朝關係史[A Historical Study of Japan−Korea Relations concerning Takeshima (Ulleungdo)](2000, Taga Publisher). Being an affair involving two countries, I criticised that the Korean side only depended on its own historical records: '一國主義的 歷

史觀'[one's own nation−centric historical view], when one should have elucidated by comparing both countries' historical documents.

Ahn Yong−bok who came to Hoki state was carrying a banner with the following inscripton: *Joulyangdo Gamsejang Sin Ahndongjigi* (朝鬱兩島監稅將臣安同知騎) [The Banner of Ahn, Joseon(Korea)'s Tax Collecting Officer for Both Islands including Ulleungdo]. Okashima Masayoshi(岡嶋正義), the official of Tottorihan, states in his *Takeshimakō*(竹嶋考), published in 1828, that 朝鬱兩島[Korea's two islands of Ulleungdo] here stands for Ulleungdo and Usando.

Further, it is still difficult to accept as a fact that Ahn Yong−bok received from the Lord of Hokihan(鳥取藩主) the document '兩島旣屬國' that appears in *Joseon Wangjo Sillok*, and confirms Ulleung and Usan were both Korean territory.

Ahn was led to the *Jōka*(城下)[an urban district outside a castle], and treated as a diplomatic envoy. Yet, he did not meet the Lord of the *Han*, so he did not receive any written confirmation(書契). One cannot deny the possibility that the petition(訴狀) was submitted to the *Shogun* via Tottorihan itself, and that the case was mentioned in this process. It can be confirmed as a fact that during the Busan negotiations the Lord of Tsushima notified the Dongrae *Busa*(府使)[magistrate] that, "Last Autumn, a person from your country submitted a petition." The Korean side also confirmed this fact saying, "It was a case of a petition made by a person who was blown (to your country) by the wind".

Thus, one must accept the fact that Ahn Yong−bok came to Tottorihan to protest, and also accept that he insisted that the two islands were Korean territory with Usando lying to the east of Ulleungdo.

5. The Meiji Government Decision

After the Meiji Restoration, the new government dispatched foreign ministry officers to Korea, and they presented a report entitled *Chōsenkoku Kōsai Shimatsu Naitansho*(朝鮮國交際 始末內探書)[An Confidential Inquiry into the Particulars of Korea's Foreing Relations] in 1870 (*Meiji* 3) on their return. The document gives details on how Takeshima and Matsushima had become Korean. Stating that, "Matsushima is an island belonging to Takeshima. There are no documents published about Matsushima and after *Genroku Jidai* (元祿時代)[*Genroku* period] some settlers were sent for a while from Korea", the report shows the realization that both Takeshima and Matsushima are Korean territory.

Subsequently, the new government faced the problem of how they were going to manage the application for the development of Takeshima or Matsushima. In the late 18th century, a western ship entered the Sea of Japan, found unmapped Takeshima and Matsushima and wanted to give them new names. One example is Smith's 'Map of Japan'(日本圖) on which Takeshima is named 'Argonaut' and Matsushima 'Dazure'. Siebold, who was in Nagasaki, confused the names of Takeshima and Matsushima, so that Ulleungdo (Takeshima) became Matsushima and Matsushima (present−day Takeshima) became Takeshima. Later, a French whaling vessel called present−day Takeshima the *Liancourt* Rocks, and this name was used on western sea maps. It became known as the Lianko Rocks in Japan as well.

Amid this confusion of names, the Japanese government felt the necessity to confirm the situation on the island and investigate by sending ships and asking Shimane Prefecture about the issue. In 1876, at the request of the government, Shimane Prefecture surveyed the historical references. The prefecture then asked the Ministry of

Home Affairs whether they could include the island located to the northwest of Oki in sphere. The Ministry of Home Affairs conducted its own independent research and came to the conclusion that there was another island, apart from Takeshima, and that was not considered Japanese territory. However, the matter of territorial jurisdiction was so important that they asked for a decision by the *Daijōkan* (太政官)[Council of the State] in March of the following year. Eventually, with the approval given by Iwakura(岩倉) the Minister of State and three other officials under him, the Home Affairs Ministry concluded that, "Takeshima and the other island had no relation to Japan."

Also, in 1880 the Hydrographic Office of the Ministry of Navy sent the battleship Amagi(天城) to conduct a survey, concluding that "It is Ulleungdo(called so in the olden days). And suddenly, a burning question of many years was answered knowing that it is merely a rock, although it is called an island in that region." This appears in Kitazawa Seisei's(北澤正誠) *Takeshima Kōshō*(竹島考証)[Research into Takeshima](1996, reprint).

6. Imperial Ordinance No. 41 of the Korean Empire

Imperial Ordinance No. 41 of the Korean Empire was issued on October 25, 1900. It stated that Ulleungdo was to be renamed Uldo. *Dogam* (chief of the Island) was to be called *Gunsu* (magistrate of a county), and the county system brought into effect. Further, Uldo County received jurisdiction over Jukdo and Seokdo, as well as Uldo. Here the Korean side argued that Jukdo is Jukseodo(竹嶼島), located near Ulleungdo, and Seokdo corresponds to Dokdo. At that time, many people in the county were from(Korea's) Jeolla Province and they spoke Jeolla dialect. Therefore they pronounced 'Dok' which means 'alone' or 'lonely'(獨) as 'Dol' meaning 'stone'(石). What was meant as Dol Island (石島/Stone Island) came to be written according to the spoken form. This is how the island came to be called Dokdo(獨島).

In relation to this, there is a story about Matsushima (present-day Takeshima) recorded on September 25, 1904 in the logbook of the battleship Niidaka(新高). It describes how a log was taken of comments made by people who had been to Matsushima and had seen the *Liancourt* Rocks first hand. It reports that, "The Korean people call the *Liancourt* Rocks Dokdo(獨島), and Japanese fishermen call them the Liankodō (Lianko Island), a contracted form." In other words, when Koreans write the island's name in Chinese letters, it appears as Dokdo(獨島), not Seokdo(石島).

Likewise, due to the fact that they recognized Seokdo as Dokdo included in Uldo County, Ganda(神西), the director of Shimane Prefecture, and his party asked Magistrate Shim Hong−taek(沈興澤) of Uldo County about the matter of incorporating Liankodō. The Magistrate of Uldo County was shocked at the news of Dokdo becoming Japanese and immediately reported this to the Gangwon Provincial Office demanding action.

If one confirms the fact that the imperial ordinance of 1900 refers to 石島[Stone Island], namely Dokdo, as Korean territory, then the 1905 Japanese incorporation of Liankodō cannot be justified by referring to it as occupation of *terra nullius*.

One cannot accept that the Japanese officials did not know that Liankodō was Korean territory. Let me list a few examples. First, Tabuchi Domohiko(田淵友彥) lists Yangkodō in his book *Kankoku Shin Chiri*(韓國新地理)[New Korean

Geography](1905) in the section on Gangwon Province. "Believing this island to be Korean", Nakai Yosaburō, who applied for the incorporation of Dokdo into Japan, came to the capital in order to submit to the Korean government an petition for a lease(奥原碧雲, 『竹島は 鬱陵島』, 1907).

The Bureau of Local Affairs of the Ministry of Home Affairs, which received the petition from Nakai, rejected the application replying that, "By taking over such barren islands, which might be territory of Korea, may amplify foreign countries' mistrust of us. This may give the impression that our country has ambitions to absorb Korea" (Vol. 1, *Takeshima Kankei Shiryō*[竹島關係資料], Shimane Prefecture Public Relations Department).

7. The Incorporation of Liankodō into Japan

In the autumn of 1904 Nakai Yosaburo of Shimane Prefecture, Saikōcho(西郷町) went to Tokyo. After his application to the Ministry of Home Affairs was turned down, he met Yamaza Enziro(山座圓次郎), the Director of Political Affairs at MOFA. Yamaza said, "The present situation really calls for incorporation as the prime objective, and there is no need to worry as the Home Affairs Ministry appears to be." Since Yamaza had worked at the legation in Seoul, he knew Korea well. Moreover, Maki Bokushin (牧朴眞), the Director of Fisheries of the Ministry of Agriculture and Commerce, discussed this affair with Kimotsuke Kaneyuki (肝付兼行), the Director of Hydrography at the Admiralty. Then they submitted the application for the 'incorporation and lease of Yankodō' to the three ministers of home affairs, foreign affairs and of agriculture and commerce. Kimotsuke (肝付), a director at the Admiralty, said, "From General Kimotsuke's(肝付) conclusions, we confirmed that this island does not belong to anyone." Referring to the fact that Nakai had begun to catch seals on Liankodō the year before, the director proposed that the island be incorporated into Japan by applying the theory of occupying *terra nullius*.

This was when the Russo–Japanese war had already started. In June, an army transport ship was sunk in the Tsushima Strait, which caused concern over the Vladivostok fleet's southwards advance. The navy decided to construct observation posts on the Korean east coast and lay a telegraph cable. In September, an undersea telegraph cable was deployed between Ulleungdo and the Korean coast. For that reason, Director Yamaza of the Ministry of Foreign Affairs built a watchtower on Liankodō(present–day Takeshima) and laid an undersea cable saying "there will be no more anxiety in terms of the surveillance of enemy ships", and also said that incorporation of territory was of immediate importance.

On January 8, 1905 the Cabinet's decision was recorded as follows.

> In the attached document the home affairs minister contemplates the matter of jurisdiction over an uninhabited island······since there are no indications that another country has claimed the uninhabited island, and······ according to related documents, it is clear that a man called Nakai Yosaburo migrated to the island in question, in year 36 of *Meiji*, to engage in fishery. Thus, the occupation has been endorsed by international law, and we move to incorporate the island in Japan···

Saying that it is unknown whom this uninhabited island belongs to is obviously a one−sided and arbitrary decision. As mentioned above, five years earlier in 1900, the Imperial Ordinance of Korea was promulgated. This would be why the Ministry of Home Affairs said "There are suspicions that the island may be Korean territory". Also, it says that Nakai really did migrate there and engaged in fishing. However, he merely put up a temporary, small house and only went to the island during the fishing season. This does not amount to what could be called migration. According to a report by the warship Tsushima, "it was a temporary stay of about 10 days." The Japanese side claimed that they incorporated Dokdo by way of occupying *terra nullius*. If Dokdo was *terra nullius*, the theory of indigenous territory cannot stand. Also, the truth about "occupation" becomes clear with the afore as well.

For these reasons the Foreign Ministry is putting forward a theory of reconfirming territorial sovereignty on its homepage. It reads: "The incorporation of Takeshima into Japanese territory by cabinet decision and Shimane Prefecture Public Notice was an act taken by Japanese government intention as a modern nation with the aim of possessing Takeshima... Since it was also published in a newspaper, the act was not conducted secretly; It was a valid undertaking."

However, the Korean side insists that occupation cannot be considered valid since Japan neither informed the countries concerned of the cabinet decision on territorial acquisition, nor published it in the official gazette. In addition, Shimane Prefecture that took the measure of incorporating Takeshima into Japanese territory had given only within–prefecture–notification.

Further, Japan claims that the island is indigenous Japanese territory. However, as seen above on two occasions in 1696 and 1877 they had decided that the island had no connection with Japan. In addition, since the Edo period they have denied that they held rights to the island. Not once did they maintain that it was under Japanese jurisdiction. That is to say that Japan never reaffirmed its intention to possess the island.

The name of the island can rather serve as an example for the Japanese side not having any vested territorial interests in the island. What caused Japan to give up calling Takeshima Matsushima, and without any questions use the name *Liancourt* Rocks coined by the French whaling ship?

The circumstances under which the new name was chosen are also strange. Consulted by Shimane Prefecture's Director of Home Affairs, the Governor of Oki replied that even if it was a mistake to name Ulleungdo Takeshima, ignoring the historic background, the new island should be named Takeshima since it was recorded as Matsushima (due to Siebold's misunderstanding). If we go by the governor's reason for naming the island, then it should not have been called Takeshima but Matsushima, and this applies likewise to the Edo period. And yet, no questions were asked in the Shimane Prefecture office, and the name 'Takeshima', as appears in the reply by the governor, were passed on to the home affairs ministry. A cabinet meeting decided on that name. Even locally there was very little awareness of the 'new island' Takeshima. Can one therefore call it Japan's indigenous territory?

In thinking about incorporating territory, one must bare in mind that Japanese military forces were stationed in Korea at the time.

I will now attempt to make this point clear. Japan declared war on Russia on February 10, 1904 and on February 23 concluded the Japan−Korea Protocol. This was after Japanese forces had landed at Incheon, entered Seoul and brought the city under military control. The Korean administration was taken over by Japan. And Japan became able to temporarily expropriate roads needed by its army. The right to station army or forces and to expropriate land were ensured. Furthermore, on May 31, the Cabinet decided on *Deahan Siseol Gangnyeong*(對韓施設綱領)[Principles Concerning Facilities in Korea], making it clear that Japanese policy intended to make Korea a protectorate. On August 22, in the first 'Japanese–Korean Agreement', the Korean government was forced to accept economic and foreign affairs advisors appointed by Japan.

Following the occupation of Dalian in January 1905 the battle of Mukden broke out in March. On January 28, just before the battle in the Sea of Japan in May, the Japanese Cabinet passed a resolution to incorporate Liankodō. The aforementioned shows that Yamaza the Director of Political Affairs at the Ministry of Foreign Affairs and Kimotsuke, the Director of Hydrography at the Admiralty, were purposefully influencing the events. The annexation of Takeshima took place in January under circumstances of war, after the Japanese military had seized control of public security in the Seoul area. Consequently, even though the Korean government may have been 'informed' of Japan incorporating Takeshima into its territory, because the circumstances were such that Korea could not have raised any objections, it is acceptable to think that Japan simply disregarded Korea from the outset. After the peace treaty between Japan and Russia was concluded, the second 'Japanese–Korean Agreement' was signed on November 17. From December

20 the Korean Residency–General was established, and Korea swiftly became a Japanese protectorate.

The 100th anniversary of the Japanese incorporation of Takeshima is also the 100th anniversary of the Japanese colonization of Korea. The Japanese incorporation of Takeshima was the first step of colonizing Korea.

8. The Unresolved Problem of Takeshima

The 1943 Cairo Declaration stipulates that Japan shall return territories seized by force. Since this excludes 'indigenous territory', Kawagami Kenzō and others began to research Takeshima, and wrote *Takeshima no Rekishi Chirikakuteki Kenkyu*(竹島の 歴史地理學的 研究)[A Study of Takeshima from a Standpoint of Historical Geography].

By issuing SCAPIN No. 677 in 1946, General Headquarters, Supreme Commander for the Allied Powers included Takeshima in an area where the Japanese government's administration ceased as far as Korea was concerned. SCAPIN No. 1033, issued in the same year, locates Takeshima outside the limits of Japanese fishing.

Some believe that the documents lost validity when the Treaty of Peace with Japan came into effect in 1952, and

Is Takeshima(竹島) Japanese indigenous Territory?

47

that Takeshima became Japanese territory as a result of the conclusion of the treaty. They argue that a document such as the above should not be construed as the final decision on matters of territorial sovereignty.

However, some argue that it is wrong to believe that the abrogation of SCAPIN No. 1033, effected three days before the treaty came into effect, automatically meant that all other directives were made void. The Korean side insists that since the only directive expressly referring to Takeshima is SCAPIN No. 667, then surely there is no reason why the peace treaty should conflict with it, and that there was no substantive change.

These problems were caused as a result of intensification of the Cold War in the Far East, and US attempted to tackle this situation.

In September 1949 the Soviet Union announced that it was in possession of nuclear weapons. In October the pro-American Republic of China was replaced by the People's Republic of China, and in 1950 the Korean War broke out. With the US-Soviet Cold War stand off spreading throughout the Far East, the US ordered Dulles, the advisor to the Department of State, to open preliminary negotiations in order to facilitate the conclusion of the Treaty of Peace with Japan. The US aimed to make Japan its ally, while the defeated nation resisted rearmament persisting with the idea of a 'peace−loving Japan'. According to Kawakami, the territorial division outlined in the draft peace agreement proceeded as part of efforts to establish "stability in the Far East."

Takeshima is shown as Korean territory until the draft dated November 2, 1949. Siebold, a political advisor stationed in Japan, noticed this and suggested to the Department of State that Takeshima be incorporated into Japan. He argued that a weather and radar facility should be installed there(Takeshima) in consideration of the security situation. This is how after the draft of December 29, 1949, Takeshima was classified as Japanese territory. At that time Great Britain and New Zealand had placed Takeshima outside Japanese territory, but Dulles' persuasion led to the final draft being ratified.

Of course Korea rebelled demanding that Takeshima be mentioned expressly. The US did not accept this stating that "one cannot consider that Korea had maintained its territorial claim." This was the result of Japanese diplomacy advocating the theory of 'Japan's inherent territory'. However, Korea was not merely looking on. Kim Dong—jo the then director of political affairs in the [Korean] Foreign Ministry said that the US had clearly excluded Takeshima from Japanese jurisdiction and "had tacitly endorsed Korean sovereignty over the island." One can say that America's double standards resulted in this issue being settled ambiguously.

The Treaty of Peace with Japan drawn up under US leadership does not refer to Takeshima. This is why the Japanese and Korean side interpret the situation differently. Therefore, in the postscript of his own book even Kawakami himself, who had worked at the Japanese Ministry of Foreign Affairs advocating the 'inherent territory' theory, found himself having to note that the Takeshima issue is, as of yet, unresolved. In the book, he hints that no answers had been found to problems pertaining to post—war history and to points of controversy over international law.

In any case, issues pertaining to historical events are as is stated in this article. Despite Kawakami's book being a good classic on Takeshima research, of course, today almost 40 years after it was published, various works have been published bringing forth much criticism of the book. The Japanese Ministry of Foreign Affairs' obsolete way of thinking and habit of ignoring such research results is inexcusable.

The Takeshima issue is a challenge for both Japan and Korea. There is an urgent need to establish a common forum to elucidate upon an objective comparison of historical sources belonging to both sides. In Korea, a collection of the Japanese side's original historical materials has already been published such as Song Byeong−gi's *Dokdo Yeongyugweon Saryoseon*(A Selection of Historical Materials on Sovereignty over Dokdo) (2004, Hallym University Asian Research Institute). Since this is a historical problem, I think it is crucial to confirm historical facts and then to start respect them.

[Original 『世界』 May 2005, pp.53−63]

An Introduction to Premodern Historical Studies on Takeshima

Ikeuchi Satoshi(池內敏)[1]

Introduction

In *Kanbun*(寛文) 7(1667), Saito Hōzen(齊藤豊仙) published
Onshū Shichō Gōki(隱州視聽合記)[Records on Observations
in Oki Province]. How to interpret his accounts in the opening chapter called *Kokudaiki*(國代記) has been the focus of
much debate. It is a matter of course that any debate on
Takeshima/Dokdo has carried political implications, since

1) Professor at Nagoya University Graduate School Literature Research Institute

the problem of this island's sovereignty has been raised in close relation with Korea−Japan talks(on diplomatic normalization). Going straight to the point, the focus of the debate was whether the '*Kono Shū*'(此州)[this province] in the phrase "Therefore Japan's northernmost border stretches until this province" refers to Ulleungdo (Takeshima in the Edo period) or whether it refers to Onshū(present−day Oki). The Japanese and the Korean government have on occasions been in stout opposition over this issue, the former saying it refers to Ulleungdo, the latter to Onshū. One can speculate that both sides may unilaterally have interpreted the texts under the influence of prevailing political currents, rather than giving interpretations based strictly upon accurate literal analysis. In addition to this, it is undeniable that emotional reactions have become mixed into the debate and that there have been analyses only loosely based on the original text.

Therefore, this article aims to reanalyze the original texts without any political bias. The following is a review of texts based on chapter 9 of *Zokuzoku Gunsyoruizyu* (續々群書類從) in volume 20 of the *Nihon Syomin Seikatsu Siryosyusei*(日本庶民生活史料集成)[Historic Records on the Life of Japanese Common People].2)

1. *Onshū Shichō Gōki*: Its Form, Contents and Terminology

Onshū Shichō Gōki comprises the following: an introduction and volume 1. *Kokudaiki*, volume 2. Shikichigun(周吉郡), volume 3. Ochigun(穏地郡) and volume 4. Chibugun(嶋前紀). The Oki State divides into Dōzen(嶋前) and Dōgo(嶋後). Volume 1. *Kokudaiki* deals with the whole state, whereas volumes 2. and 3. deal with Shikichigun and Ochigun belonging to Dōgo. Together with descriptions of each of their geographic features, volumes 2. and 3. also list all countryside regions, villages and hamlets, and record places of interest, ruins and local historical facts. Likewise, volume 4. lists Dōzen's Chibugun, and districts and records regions, villages and hamlets in Amabegun(海部郡). *Engikakusiki Zinmyocho* (延喜格式神名帳), *Kokuchūbuzuji*(國中佛寺), *Meisyowaka* (名所和歌), *Chibugun Takubiyama Engi*(知夫郡燒火山緣 起), *Fungakuron*(文覺論) are also included here.[3]

---

2) According to the bibliographical introduction, *Nihon Syomin Seikatsu Siryosyusei* mentioned here is a revision of 西鄉町佐々木章家傳來本, which was collated from 出雲文庫刊行會本[a translation of *Zokuzoku Gunsyoruizyu* (this is the main source)] and 隱岐鄉土研究會刊行會本(1963)[a translation of a duplicate of 西鄉町服部家藏本 (this text being the supporting source)].

3) The *Nihon Syomin Seikatsu Siryosyusei* version has a slightly different form with *Meishowaka*(名所和歌) from vol.4 appearing at the end of the document. There is also an extra map of Dōgo and Dōzen attached.

Unlike volumes 2−4, which give an itemized list of the administrative principalities, one can say that volume 1 *Kokudaiki* records characteristics and features on a national level. In order to verify the information listed in *Kokudaiki*, I will quote the rather long historical texts with added commas or spaces in order to make them more easily understandable.

[Source 1]4)

隱州在二北海中一故[云]5)　隱岐嶋（割注）「按、倭訓海

---

4) Note 2 refers to the difference between the *Zokuzoku Gunsyoruizyu* and the *Nihon Syomin Seikatsu Siryosyusei* versions. Apart from this, *Onshū Shichō Gōki* in Seoul National University Library(from now on mentioned as the Seoul University copy) was reviewed, and phrases that can be found in the Seoul University copy but cannot be found in the two previous copies were put into [ ]. Also the difference in place names and their pronunciation appearing on the maps (the maps of 嶋前 嶋i後) included were omitted. There is a red seal stating: *Keisaiteiikokudaigaku Toshoshō*(京城帝國大學圖書章) on the reverse of the Seoul University copy, and another stating *Hijinozōsho* (肱野臧書) on the cover [of the first 丁]. It is registered under application number 4710−172. At the end of the volume, "隱州視聽合記之書, 愚何幸見之, 仍爲廻嶋使理令臨寫焉, 勿論文字不正其儘而, 嶋前別府署於小各亭, 崑亨和二年壬戌冬陽復之月某日也" is written in a different handwriting. There is also the signature '井專方' and 2 seals '井專方印' '林亭'.

5) In *Onshū Shichō Gōki* cited on page 50 of Kawakami Kenzō's(川上健三) book *Takeshima no Rekishi Chiri teki Kenkyu*(竹島の歴史地理學的研究)[A Study of Takeshima from a Standpoint of Historical Geography], *Un*(云) has been inserted between '故' and '隱岐島'. Kawakami says that he quoted '云' from the 9th section of Chiribu(地理部)[the chapter on geography] in *Zokuzoku Gunsyoruizyu*, but the historical document my article refers to, does not contain the '云'. This is also the case with the *Nihon Syomin Seikatsu Siryosyusei* version. Since Kawakami also noted in the annotations that there is a copy of *Onshū Shichō Gōki* held in the cabinet archives, the historical

中言二遠幾－故名歟」6) 其在二異地－言二島前－也、

知夫郡〔チフリ〕・海部郡〔アマ〕屬レ焉、 其位二震地－7)－言二島後－、

周吉郡〔シキチ〕・穩地郡〔オチ〕屬レ焉、 其府者周吉郡南岸西鄉豊崎

也、 從レ是南[ノ方]至二雲州美穗關－三十五里、 辰巳

[ノ方] 至二伯州赤碕浦－四十里、 未申至二石州溫泉津－

五十八里、 自レ子至レ卯無レ可レ往地－、 戌亥間行二日

一夜有二松島－、 又一日程有二竹島－ (割注)「俗言二磯竹島

－、 多竹・魚・海鹿－、 [按、神言所謂五十猛歟8)]」・ 此二

二島無レ人之地、 見二高麗－如下自二雲州－9)望中隱岐

上10)、 然則日本之乾地、 以二此州－爲レ限矣、

---

records he cited might be a cabinet archives version. If this is the case, then the version in the cabinet archives is similar to the Seoul National University version. I should state here that *Onshū Shichō Gōki* referred to in a large number of works was actually cited from Kawakami's works.

6) In *Nihon Syomin Seikatsu Siryosyusei*, 名歟 is included in the main text. The Seoul National University version reads not 歟(寫) but 歟.

7) The character 震 is replaced by 靈 in the *Zokuzoku Gunsyoruizyu* version. In referring to 島前 as 異地, the character 震 in *Nihon Syomin Seikatsu Siryosyusei* fits as a corresponding phrase. Although there is some room for doubt concerning its actual location (whether south or west), it is another matter whether Dōgo(島後) actually lies to 震(the east) of 隱岐嶋(Oki Islands). Answers to this point in question will be deferred for the present.

8) In *Onshū Shichō Gōki* quoted in Kawakami's texts, there is a part referring to [ ]. It does not say 神言, but it says 神書. See footnote No. 4.

9) 雲州 is referred to as 雲岐 in *Zokuzoku Gunsyoruizyu*. As far as I see, there is no instance of 隱岐 being contracted to 岐. Also, seeing 隱岐 from 雲岐(出雲·隱岐) doesn't make any sense. Therefore, we are following the *Nihon Syomin Seikatsu Siryosyusei* version.

10) 隱岐 is replaced with 隱州 in the Seoul National University version.

民部図帳曰、凡諸健兒免ニ徭役一、隱岐國以ニ國造田三
町地子一充レ之、然近代所レ賊毎年一萬千六百余斛、其
余又以二漆・椿實（キノミ）・山椒・紫藻（ノリ）・鯛・鰯・鱝（トビウ）・鯖・石欠明（アハビ）・
烏賊（イカ）・馬皮等一、是慶長年中堀尾氏之所レ定也、

古老云曰、昔對馬守源義親之國也、其後薩摩守忠教在
二雲州美保關一領之（割注）「忠度城跡在ニ三保一」、其後
鎌倉右大將家使下ニ地頭[11]人一治上之、(中略)嗚呼此何
年、始封以來四百八十余年、時永録某年七月、其後自
ニ芸州一使下ニ猪頭九郎・岡野木工等一守中護于此上也、
此時始置二館於矢尾一居レ之、後経ニ三十八年一、毛利氏
去、堀尾氏領レ之、過二二世三十五年一而亡、又京極若
州大守領レ之、一世四年而亡、遂歸二萬々世一矣

Mentioned above, *Kokudaiki* is composed of approximately three parts. "隱州在二北海中" to "然則日本之乾地以此州爲限矣" list the geographic characteristics of Oki State. Parts "民部図帳日" to "是慶長年中堀尾氏之所レ定也" list the tributary taxes levied on Oki State. Finally, parts "古老云曰" to "遂歸二萬々世一矣" are records of Oki State's history (records on changes of warlords who ruled Oki State that stretched from 源義親 to 京極).

Although the text forms three parts, up until now any

---

11) The character 字 is referred to as 領 in *Zokuzoku Gunsyoruizyu*.

analyses focused only on the first part, which mentions geographical features. This part was analyzed without referring to the rest of the chapter entitled *Kokudaiki* or indeed even to the rest of the whole book *Onshū Shichō Gōki*. It is unnatural to think that Saito Hōsen's(齊藤豊仙) writing stance or the first part of his writing is independent from the rest of the book. To understand his intentions or the contents of his writing, it is absolutely necessary to analyze the writing style in the other parts of *Kokudaiki* and the whole of the book *Onshū Shichō Gōki* in their entirety.

If so, the first part, which is a major point of the issue, must be deciphered as follows. Because the debate is split over the interpretation of the word 州 in the word 此州, for the moment it shall be transcribed as only 州.

(1-1) Since Oki State is located in the middle of the northern sea, it is called Oki Island. On reflection, the middle of the sea is called 遠幾(Oki) in *Wakun*(倭訓). Is that where the name of Oki State originates from?

(1-2) (In Oki State) The island located in the south—east (of the Oki Islands) is called Dōzen. Chibugun and Amagun belong here.

(1-3) (In Oki State) It says the island in the east is called Dōgo. Shikichigun and Ochigun belong here.

(1-4) The 府(capital) (of Oki State) is Saigo Toyozaki (西鄉 豊崎) on the south coast of Shikichigun.

(2-1) It is 35 *ri*(里) from the south (of Oki State) to Izumokuni(出雲國) and Mihoseki(美穗關).

(2-2) Akasakiura(赤崎浦) in Hokikuni(伯耆國) is 40 *ri* to the south−east (of Oki State).

(2-3) Onsenzu(溫泉津) in Iwamikuni(石見國) is 58 *ri* to the south−west (of Oki State).

(2-4) There is no land to the north and east (of Oki State).

(2-5-1) If one travels two days and one night in the direction between *Jutsu*(戌, west−northwest) and *Gai*(亥, north−northwest), which is approximately the direction of the north−west, one will arrive at Matsushima.

(2-5-2) If one travels another day from there (Matsushima), there is Takeshima. Commonly called Isotakeshima(磯竹島), it has a lot of bamboo, fish and sea lions.[Considering this, could it be *Isotake*(五十猛) referred to in the so-called *Shingen*(神言)?]

(2-5-3) As these two islands (Matsushima and Takeshima) are uninhabited, seeing Oki from Unshū(雲州) is the same as seeing Goryeo (Korea) from there.

(3) If this is the case, then this *Shū*(州) is the north-western limit of Japan.

As mentioned above, it is clear that the first part of *Kokudaiki* is describing geographical characteristics in three parts; 1-1 to 1-4 are about the make up of Oki State; 2-1 to 2-5 describe what surrounds Oki State in all directions; and based on the whole of section (2), (3) describes Oki's location in relation to the Japanese mainland. As mentioned previously, *Kokudaiki* describes in three parts Oki's geography, tribute and history as that of a country. Since part (3) summarized above is placed immediately before another item(concerning tributes), it corresponds to the closing part giving an account of Oki State as a country unit. In light of these facts, if one wishes to interpret these historical records as they are, it becomes clear what "this prefecture(此州)" indicates, and cannot be subject of any controversy.

Nevertheless, the debate has not come to a conclusion. Reason for this endless controversy appears to be the contention that 州 might as well be replaced and read as 島 (嶋). I think this argument derives from Tagawa Kōzō[田川孝三, p. 43] saying 州 means 'island' (州はシマの意である).[12] The primary cause of this confusion lies with the fact that this opinion merely reiterates itself over and over again without reexamining its basis.[13]

---

12) This sentence by Tagawa Kōzō appears in the article 'An Enquiry into the Sovereignty of Takeshima' carried in 東洋文庫書報 No. 20 published in 1988. Said thesis would have been written much earlier than the date of publishing, as it was an 'unpublished paper chosen' and put into 東洋文庫書報 after Tagawa Kōzō's death in October 1988. However, this quote appears in the paper; "The view concerning Takeshima presented by the Korean government sofar has entirely been a counter argument to our government's position. It is no more than a persistent repetition of the fragmented position that has been presented earlier before.···(omitted) ··· below, I shall express my own opinion while criticizing the Korean standpoint" (p.6).

最近、韓國が提示してきた同國政府の竹島に關する見解は、專らこれ迄のわが國政府の見解に對する反論に終始しており、從來よりの彼の見解の一部を繰返えし主張しているにすぎない。…(中略)…以下、彼が主 張を批判しつつ、所見を述べよう(六頁)

13) Shimojō Masao argues that there is no problem with referring to 此州 as Ulleungdo(鬱陵島) since 州 carries the meaning of 島(island), and 隱岐島 seems to be called '隱州'. Even Lee Ik(李瀷) records the fact that Ulleungdo was reclaimed by Korea thanks to Ahn Yong−bok's distinguished service [to Korea] by writing: "because it says restoring a province's land" (一州の

The following list shows examples of how 州 and 島(嶋) are used in *Onshū Shichō Gōki*. When looking at the usage of 州, there are 66 instances found in *Onshū Shichō Gōki*. One finds that 60 examples abbreviate specific country names such as Oki State and Izumo State as Onshū(隱州), Unshū(雲州). The sentences preceding and following the remaining six instances are discussed below in order of appearance (the underlined are quotes,...).

A 戌亥間行二日一夜有二松島一、又一日程有二竹島一、
此二島無レ人之地、見二高麗一如下自二雲州一望中隱岐

土を復す) (Shimojō Masao 1996, p.50). It is also a mistake to read "just as calling the Oki Islands Onshū (隱岐島を隱州とするように)." That is to say Oki State (隱岐國) should be called Onshū(隱州), not the Okishima(隱岐島)[Oki Islands] Onshū(隱州)[Oki Province]. There must be people who read "隱州在 北海中 故隱岐島" in the first part of Kokudaiki and immediately raise an objection saying, "Look, 州 and 島(嶋) have been mixed up, haven't they?!." Yet, this objection has no basis. Below, I quote the first few lines appearing after the opening part, except for those not necessary for this discussion.

隱州在 北海中 故隱岐島, 其(1)在 巽地 言 島前 也, 知夫郡海部
郡屬 焉 其(2)位 震地 言 島後, 周吉郡穩地郡屬焉, 其(3)府者周吉
郡南岸西鄉豊崎也,(remainder omitted)

As seen above, the indicative pronoun 其(that) appears three times between other lines after "隱州在 北海中 故隱岐島"(Underlined ①-③). Seen in the context one can only think that ①-③ all take the same preceding proper noun. Further the proper noun in question can only be either Onshū or Okishima. Concerning instances ① and ② either Onshū or Okishima are possible. In case ③ Okishima is not possible, because 府 refers to 國府(=國衙). For this reason, ③ can only be linked to Oki Kuni隱岐國(Oki State)..Therefore one cannot exchange read 州 as 島(嶋) in the above passage.

An Introduction to Premodern Historical Studies on Takeshima

上、然則日本之乾之地、以二此州一爲レ限矣、
(『續々群書類從』第九、四五〇頁上段)

B 雲州刺史海尼子伊予守者、佐々木之棟梁、隣州之盟
主也 (同前四五〇頁下段)

C 聞二元就欲下討二隱州一…（中略）…爲清之旧臣(個人
名五人省略)潛偶語而曰、清家二雖令弟一本比肩之家
人 (也)、五郎郡雖二幼弱一佐々木之根本也、以二才
又郎一仮二元就威一以至二此州一則五儕皆渠之馬卒也
(同前、四一五頁上段ー下段、なお「」内は『日本
庶民生活史料集成』による)

D 一國悉奉二五郎君一爲二主君一、寺本等威權行二內外
一、莫下曾達二於心一者上、才又郎在二芸州一聞レ之、
泣告二元就一曰、我生不レ可レ戴レ天、若以二君之靈一賜
二命世上一、乃請勞二二百騎一、自則招二旧交人一對二
隱州一、以二其地一爲二付庸一長守二藩屏一、言與レ淚
俱也、元就憫レ之以二百余騎一與レ之、才又郎大悅到
二雲州笠浦一、覘二於隱州動靜一、雖レ然風波難レ期空
迻二數日一、此時一州人以二五郎君之年少一晨夕遊宴
軍制相忘、不レ門二津口之出入一也、
(同前、四五二頁、上段)

E 昔鄭交題二古塚一曰、塚上雨竿「竹」、風吹常
裊々、塚中有レ聲曰一、下有二百年人一長睡不レ知レ
曉于レ漢于レ和有レ似矣哉、又此州之老或有下称二村

上天皇之末孫−而号中村上某上問三其所二由出一則
曰、唐之遣腹也、(同前、四六一頁下段、なお　「」
內は『日本庶民生活史料集成』本による)

F　其沖に松島あり、上に松生て樹間に荒園あり、長事
　　二町ばかり、昔好事者此州に雉の無事を愁て、誠に
　　雲州より雌雄を渡して此に放つ、一年を経て終に亡
　　と云（同前四六五頁下段）

A-D above are statements included in volume 1 of
Kokudaiki. E and F are statements included in *Kaminisizato*
(上西里) and *Takugiura*(硝木浦) of volume 2 Dōgo(島後)
Shikichigun respectively. Let us examine these six cases
divided into 4 examples where '此州' appears (in A, C,
E and F), and the remaining two examples (B"隣州," D"一
州").

This section will investigate the latter first. In B, 隣州
can mean "the Izumo state nearby Oki State" based on
Izumo's *Shishi*(刺史)[*Kuninokami*(國守), a local official
sent by the central government, a governor], which mentions that Amako Iyonokami(尼子伊予守) was the *Tōryō*
(棟梁[chief]) of the Sasaki(佐々木) tribe, as well as the
Meishu(盟主[leader]) of 隣州. Here, the 州(prefecture)
means 國(state). D cannot be understood without being
aware of the political circumstances surrounding Oki

State, recorded in *Senkokuki*(戰國期) [The Nation at War] in *Kokudaiki*. "After the death of Sasaki Damekiyo(佐々木爲淸) who was ruling the whole of Oki as a nation, his son Koro(五郎) was so young that the Damekiyo's brother Kiyoie(淸家) took Sasaki Damekiyo's position as ruler of Oki. Saimataro(才又郎), the son of Kiyoie, became Mori Motonari's(毛利元就) guarantee. Teramoto(寺本), the old liegeman of the Sasaki family, did not like to serve under Kiyoie who had once been their comrade, and confronted Kiyoie and Saimataro in the name of his young ward, Koro. Saimataro who was away in Akikoku (安芸國)[Aki State] appealed to Motonari, borrowed army forces and arrived in Izumo. At that time, "the people of 一州" or more precisely the people of Oki State, defended the nation negligently because Koro was so young." By reading through the quote one can find that political trends of each state such as Aki(安芸), Unshū(雲州) and Onshū(隱州) were recorded. The 一州 in the first sentence of the quotation means the same as 一國, and indicates Oki State. The 州 here has the same meaning as 國, nation.

Next, let us examine the four sections(A · C · E · F) which use 此州. As A is the focus of the debate we shall leave it aside for now. Section C is a record from a slightly earlier period than D. "With a rumour threatening an imminent attack on Oki by Mori Motonari, the liegemen following the dead lord's son Koro are afraid of being treated as common soldiers by their former kinsmen should Saimataro gain power from Motonari and attack 此州. Although there is no proper noun nearby for the 此州(meaning "this 州") to refer to, one can infer from the context that Oki is meant. Passage E appears in the quote beginning with "昔鄭交題二古塚一曰" in the chapter under the title Kaminisizato(上西里) in volume 2. Dōgo Shikichigun. In this section there is no suitable pronoun referring to the '此'(meaning 'this') in 此州. In passage F, there is no proper noun answering to the '此' in '此州'. Supposing that 州 meant 島(island) and that 此州 is the nearby Matsushima, then the report in 昔好事者 could be read as follows: "A long time ago a curious man thought it sad that there were no pheasants on Matsushima. As a trial, he took some pheasants from Izumo and left them on Matsushima, only to find that they had all disappeared a year later(breeding had failed)." However, if there were no pheasants on this island off the coast of Takukiura village in the Shikichi region of Dōgo County(within Oki), then bringing them from the far away Izumo State rather than taking pheasants from somewhere else in Oki sounds unnatural. Seeing that they brought pheasants from Izumo(the eastern part of today's Shimane Prefecture) because there were none on 此州, would logically suggest that Onshū (隱州)[Oki State] is meant and that Matsushima cannot possibly be 此州. Therefore 州 can not be understood as meaning 'island'.

The above analysis points out the common points in the passages C, E and F. No proper noun corresponds to the demonstrative pronoun 此('this'), or at least there is none close enough nearby. Nevertheless, as this is obvious in E to begin with, people reading these sentences might have understood them anyway even though there is no proper noun referring to 此州. For the words 此州 were used in the books entitled *Onshū Shichō Gōki*.

Whether looking at short sections of the text or at the whole, the writing is about 隱州(Oki State). Since we have understood this idea, even though there is no proper noun close by referring to it, the 此州 can be read as indicating 隱州. Another matching part in passage E reads: "There is among the elderly of Oki a man going by the name Murakamibō(村上某)[Murakami so−and−so] known as a descendent of the Emperor Murakami(村上). When asked about details, he said that he is the posthumous son of Karahashi(唐橋)[Karahashi Chūshō(唐橋中將)·Minamotono Masakio(源雅清)]." So he was recognized as a descendent of the Emperor Murakami.[14]

Meanwhile, "there are 29 cases where 島(嶋) is used but does not mean 'island'. Apart from these, there is a great number of cases (76) where it is used as a particular island name. A further 22 cases only relate without exception to words referring to islands as 小陸地[small areas of land] "places surrounded by water" (Kōzien[廣辭苑] from paragraph 島, 嶋).

Yet, under examples classified as exceptions there are five instances indicating 此. The following section deals with these briefly.

G 津戸に渡る半に篷島と云あり、皆大岩なり、昔津戸、蛸木<u>此島</u>をあらそふ (『續々郡書類從』第九、四五〇頁上段、卷二、島後周吉郡「蛸木浦」項)

H 海路半を過て大守島と云有、東西三町計、岩間有

14) The section titled Kaminisizato(上西里) documents a legend about Karahashi Chūshō(Minamotono Masakio) who was banished to Oki, first stayed in Husemura(布施村), Dōgo and later moved to Kaminisato where he died.

りて舟を倚す、或は風起潮渦まく時は<u>此島</u>ニ舟を倚て生を得者多し,（同前、四六七頁上段、巻三、島前穏地郡「津戸」項）

I 河の南に見付嶋と云あり、蓋埼村より入來る船の先づ<u>此嶋</u>を見に依り、（同前、四七四頁上段、巻四、島前知夫郡「知夫郡」頁）

J 岸を離れて五町ばかり南の沖に基島あり、廻り十町ばかり、其上に竹を産す故に竹島とも云、西風厲しく潮煙常に灌ぎかゝる、此故に竹の色班々として節高からず、葉も又短し、好事の者此を求る事多し、然ども四面絶壁にして而も林中蛇多し、若此島に至らんと欲者は風浪の穏なるを窺ひ孤舟に乗て岸に至り（同前、四七七頁下段、巻四、島前知夫郡　「知夫湊」項）

It is clear that 此島(嶋)[this island] appearing in passages G−J refers to Tomashima(篷島) in G, Ōmorishima(大守島) in H, Mitsukeshima(見付嶋) in I and (Takeshima [Motoshima])−(竹島[基島]) in J. It is also obvious that the aforenamed cases of 此二島(嶋)[these two islands] in passage A mean Matsushima(松島) and Takeshima(竹島). Therefore the part preceding the indicator 此二島 must be an island name of its own.

As a result of investigating all the instances of 州 and 島(嶋) appearing in the text Onshū Shichō Gōki, one may conclude that among the 66 cases of '州' used in the whole text, excluding passage A, the remaining 65 are used in the sense of 國(nation). The analysis also indicates that when one tries to refer again to a particular island by using the words including the indicator '此', one uses the word 此島(嶋).[15] In other words when the text refers to an island name of its own, the word 此州 (this island) is not used.

So, if we accept this premise, then part A, put aside before, cannot but be read as "then the northwestern end of Japan is Okishū(Oki State)."

Looking at the sentence construction and terminological characteristics leads to the same conclusion. Nevertheless, to say that one must accept that '此州' in A should be interpreted as meaning 島(嶋) is unreasonable and cannot but be criticized as arbitrary.

---

15) Occasionally, as the below mentions, one can notice cases in which only a word '此' refer to preceding indigenous island names(固有島名): "從是して 篷島と号す、今俗此を前平島と号するは…" (『續々群書類從』第九、四六六頁上段)、「東北の海中に小竹島あり、此より海部の崎村に渡ること海路一里五町」(同前、四七なな頁下段)、「又北に二股島二幷ひて大岩の出たるあり、此を新島と云」"

2. Considering the theory that 此州 refers to Takeshima(Ulleungdo)

(1) How to read *Onshū Shichō Gōki*

It is also historical fact that arguments took place over the interpretation of *Kokudaiki* in *Onshū Shichō Gōki* while the Korean and Japanese governments were exchanging opinions on the return of Takeshima/Dokdo. Here, among the opinions expressed, we turn to Tsukamoto Takashi's(塚本 孝) summary to analyze the debate surrounding the interpretation of the historic materials in question.

First of all, at the time of the first exchange of views on the matter, neither the Japanese government's position, stated July 13, 1953, nor the Korean position given on September 9 of the same year referred to any historical documents at all. Next, the Japanese first quoted an historical source *Onshū Shichō Gōki* in a statement made on February 2, 1954. On September 25 that same year, the Korean side simply said that *Onshū Shichō Gōki* was "invalid as evidence." Both the Japanese and the Korean governments did not touch upon issues concerning the interpretation of *Onshū Shichō Gōki*.[16)]

16) The sections of the Japanese position dated February 19, 1954 relating to

On September 20, 1956 the Japanese government stated they were of the opinion that, "The 1667 *Onshū Shichō Gōki* reports Matsushima(present−day Takeshima) and Takeshima(Ulleungdo) as the north−western border of Japan." This view is presented briefly but concretely (Tsukamoto Takashi, p.53). The Korean government's counter−argument against this Japanese view was presented as follows in the Korean government's statement of January 7, 1959.

Japan quoted *Onshū Shichō Gōki* in order to strengthen

Onshū Shichō Gōki are as follows. "Takeshima has been known to the Japanese from a long time ago under the name of Matsushima and was considered part of Japanese territory. Further, it is a place Japanese sailed to in order to fish. Especially, during the *Iemizu*(家光) period of the Tokugawa family, the Ooya and Murakawa families of Yonago sailed to Takeshima after they had received permission to control the island from the *Shogunate*. They always fished there as well as used this island as a stop on the way. Documents referring to the above fact are *Onshū Shichō Gōki* compiled in 1667 by Saito Moshi(齋藤某氏[Mr. saito so−and−so])an official of Izumohan, and the memoirs of Ooya *Kyūemon Kazunobu*(大谷九右衛門勝信) written in the 19th year of 延保(天和 1, 1681). Also there are maps referring to the above fact. These maps are Takeshimazu(竹島圖) owned in the 1720s by Iketa family, Lord of Tottorihan, and Nihonyoshi Roteizenzu(日本與地路程全圖) by Nagakubo Sekisui(長久保赤水) written in *Onei*(安永) 4th year(1775)."[Tsukamoto, p.60]. The following is the Korean government position of August 25 that year: "The Japanese government invokes '*Onshū Shichō Gōki*' (1667) and the memoirs of Ooya Kyūemon (1681) as evidence proving their right to Dokdo. As these documents were written during the Japanese invasions of Ulleungdo (1614−1697), the Korean government regards them invalid as proof."(Tsukamoto Takashi, p.54) their claims. However, they have seriously misinterpreted its contents. This book says Onshū(prefecture) is Japan's north-western border. Here is the original text:

隱州在北海中　故云隱岐嶋 (割注)「按倭訓海中言遠故名与」
南方至雲州美穗關　戌亥間行二日一夜有松島　又一日程有竹島　此二島無人之地　見高麗如自雲州望隱州　然則日本之乾地以此州爲限矣

The Matsushima mentioned here refers to Dokdo, and Takeshima refers to Ulleungdo. Looking at Goryeo (Korea) from these two islands is the same, in terms of distance, as looking at Onshū from Unshū, so that this Shū is the north-western border of Japan. Seeing Goryeo's(Korea's) mainland from these two islands is just like seeing Inshū from Onshū. Thus, this prefecture constitutes the north-western border of Japan. Japan made a mistake when saying "both islands are Japan's north-western border." The writer of *Onshū Shichō Gōki* presented the matter correctly (Tsukamoto Takashi, p.56).

The Japanese government made no official reply to the Korean statement above, and *Onshū Shichō Gōki* was never again made subject of discussion between them.[17]

---

17) Zukamoto Takashi revealed the following about the Korean government

However, when considering the above account, one realizes that *Onshū Shichō Gōki* had been read with two things in mind. Firstly, it is the first record to call Takeshima/Dokdo Matsushima (A). Secondly, it is a written reference describing Japan's north−western border in the latter part of the 17th century (B). Further concerning (B), the interpretations of the sentence "日本之乾地以此州爲限矣" surfaced as a problem. Therefore, this article will investigate how this historical source has been interpreted chronologically over a longer period of time, not merely during 1954−59 when Japan and Korea exchanged views referring to *Onshū Shichō Gōki*.

"Various points" referred to in *Onshū Shichō Gōki*, appended to this section, is an attempt by the author to collate as long a list of arguments as possible referring to *Onshū Shichō Gōki*. Among the materials listed there, those concerning *Onshū Shichō Gōki* were extracted and are arranged (below) in order of publication.

After reading this list all the way through, one finds that there were approximately 20 statements made concerning (A) between the 1906 statement by Okuhara

---

view in an annotation: "The Japanese government did not directly reply to this criticism."

Hekiun(奥原碧雲) and the 2001 view expressed by Shin Yong-ha. All these studies hold the same view, namely that the first Japanese document calling Takeshima/Dokdo Matsushima is the historical source *Onshū Shichō Gōki.*

Further to this, there are various discrepancies concerning point (B). These can be explained by analyzing the opposing views presented in (I) and (II), and the statements deriving from them (I)', (II)' and (III)'' in the following list.

(I) Ulleungdo(then called Takeshima) was considered the north-western border of Japanese territory in the mid-17th century.

(II) The Oki State(Oki Island) was considered the north-western border of Japanese territory in the mid-17th century.

(I)' Ulleungdo(Takeshima) and Takeshima/Dokdo were considered Japanese territory in the mid-17th century.

(II)' Ulleungdo(Takeshima) and Takeshima/Dokdo were not considered Japanese territory in the mid-17th century.

(II)" Ulleungdo(Takeshima) and Takeshima/Dokdo were considered Chosen(Korean) territory in the mid-17th century.

Among those found to be following theory (I) are: Okuhara Hekiun in 1906, Tagawa Kōcho from the late 50s to early 60s (one assumes), Ookuma Ryōichi(大熊良一) in 1968, Shimojō Masao(下條正男) in 1996, Naitō Seichū(內藤正中) in 2000 and Shimojō Masao in 2004 as well as the Japanese government in September 1956.[18] Those shown following opinion (I)' are the Research Department of the Ministry of Foreign Affairs (Kawakami Kenzō was the author) in 1953 and Hwang Sang-gi in 1952.

---

18) Strictly speaking, there is a difference between these opinions, namely that the Japanese government considers the two islands, Ulleungdo and the present-day Takeshima, the north-western border of Japan, whereas the others consider only Ulleungdo the border. Note here that, the Japanese government read the text as saying "the north-western border of Japan is Matsushima (present-day Takeshima) and Takeshima (Ulleungdo)." However this statement was analyzed incorrectly, because although in the words 此州, the 此, meaning 'this', is a singular demonstrative pronoun modifying '州', the Japanese government thought '此' modifies a plural noun. This is an outrageous mistake.
 Again, the Korean government counters this Japanese government view by invoking the phrase "Looking at Goryeo(Korea) mainland... from the distance of..". This counter-argument by the Korean government is also a misinterpretation that resulted from the above Japanese government's misinterpretation.

On the other side are those making statements agreeing with opinion (II): Hwang Sang-gi in 1957 and 1965; Lee Han-gi in 1969; Kajimura Hideki in 1978; Song Byeong-gi, Choi Seok-u and Paek Chung-hyeon all in 1989 and 1991; Shin Yong-ha in 1996; Lee Hoon, Gwak Chang-gon and Kim Byeong-ryeol all in 1996; again Shin Yong-ha in 2001 and the Korean government in January, 1959. Those making statements agreeing with (II)" are Song Byeon-gi and Paek Chung-hyeon in 1985. Opinion (II)" appealed to Hwang Sang-gi (a) in 1965; Shin Yong-ha in 1989, 1991, 1996a, 1996b; Lee/Yi Hun in 1996, and again Shin Yong-ha in 2001.

Let us first turn to theory (II) and examine the grounds for interpreting 此州 as meaning 隱州. If one considers the statements: "if read carefully......is obvious" (Lee Hun) or "contextually and logically sound" (Kim Byeong-ryeol) not enough of an explanation, then the opinions by Hwang Sang-gi (1965b): "because 隱州 is the main object," or Gwak Chang-gon's: the words 隱州 appearing at the begin-ning as the main theme of the report (*Onshū Shichō Gōki*) refer to the prefecture name(州名) which precedes 此州, can be called concrete.

Table 1. Uses of '州' and '島(嶋)' in *Onshū Shichō Gōki*.

The uses of '州'	
國代記	36 specified names of countries: (隱州11, 雲州11, 芸州6, 若州3, 伯州2, 但州2, 石州) 此州2, 隣州, 一州
卷2 以後	24 specified names of countries: (隱州9, 雲州7, 伯州3, 因州, 但州, 勢州, 若州, 豆州) 此州2
計	60 specified names of countries: 此州4, 隣州, 一州

The uses of '島(嶋)'/island(isles)	
國代記	12 geographical names that can not necessarily be categorized as 'names of islands': (島前6, 島後4, 島根郡2) 4 specified names of islands: (隱岐島, 松島, 竹島, 磯竹島) Other: 2(此二島, 孤島)
卷 2 以後	17 geographical names that can not necessarily be categorized as 'names of islands': (島前7, 島後4, 新島守2, 島崎, 島神, 島地, 敷島) 72 specified names of islands: (松島3, 白島3, 渡島2, 磯竹島2, 冠島2, 籬島2, 白戶島2, 篷島2, 赤島2, 小峰島2, 黑島2, 長島, 靑島, 鷗島, 中島, 甲島, 琴島, 小敷島, 烏帽子島, 鴉島, 小白島, 帆掛島, 屛島, 田島, 沖

	島, 左婦島, 姫島, 雀島, 鶴島, 具島, 平島, 神島, 前平島, 大形島, 賤木島, 大守島, 宇津島, 柱島, 神의島, 恩部島, 平瀬島, 大領島, 巫島, 見付島, 立島, 膝島, 雁島, 麻島, 駄島, 伊島, 犬島, 津目島, 基島, 竹島, 小竹島, 三郎島, 小守島, 二股島, 新島)(*) Others: 19 (島7, 小島5, 此島4, 一島, 孤島, 最遠島)
計	29 geographical names that can not necessarily be categorized as 'names of islands'. 76 geographical names specified names of islands. Others: 21

Notes

Numbers represent amounts of cases, no number means only one occurrence.

(*) 面例御島 appears as the name of an island in the article 續々郡書類從. However it appears as 面洲御岐 in the Nihon Syomin Seikatsu Siryosyusei version. Here I follow the latter, so I do not treat it as the name of an island.

(2) Arguments supporting the idea that 此州 means Ulleungdo (1)

Tagawa Kōjō, Shimojō Masao and Naitō Seichū are among those supporting opinion (I), mentioned above, stating that 此州 actually designates Ulleungdo.

First we turn to what Tagawa Kōjo states about paying attention to the conjunction 然則(because of this reason) in the phrase "然則日本之乾地, 以二此州一爲レ限矣." Let us first turn to Tagawa Kōjō who said the following, drawing attention to the conjunction 然則 in the phrase "然則日本之乾地, 以二此州一爲レ限矣."

> Seeing Goryeo(Korea) from Takeshima is the same as seeing Onshū(隱州) from Unshū(雲州). As stated above, this shū/'州'(州 here meaning island) must be considered the 乾方[north−western] border of Japan. Therefore what has been written in the various books and maps previously is based on this meaning (Tagawa Kōjo, pp.42−43).

This historical source explicates that "Seeing Goryeo is the same as seeing Onshū from Unshū. Therefore, Japan's territory ends with this 州." Here, about the location from which the text describes "seeing Goryeo," the Korean government's interpretation of the statement "seeing Goryeo mainland from these two islands[Ulleungdo and Takeshima/Dokdo]"(see footnote 17) should be revised to "seen from Ulleungdo(Takeshima)." However, because only the sentences immediately preceding and following the words 然則 were read, it was mistakenly assumed that 此州 and 見高麗 shared the same subject. Therefore, they could not but read 州 as meaning 島.

But, among the materials quoted above, "many books of 從前[before]" and 'the map' Tagawa referred to are *Onshū Shichō Gōki* and Okubo Sekisui's *Nihon Yochi Rotei Zenzu*(日本輿地路程全図)(an annotation in these texts concerning Takeshima). These documents record that the Korean Peninsula could definitely be seen from Takeshima(Ulleungdo).[19] However, this merely confirms that Takeshima(Ulleungdo) and Goryeo as well as Izumo and Oki lie within a range of view respectively. Nowhere does it describe Takeshima(Ulleungdo) being part of Japanese territory. The phrase "therefore, one must take this 州, forming Japan's west−northern border(乾方)" merely reveals the author's own assumptions.

Generally speaking there is some sense in reading 州 as meaning 島(an island). In all events, without any ob-

---

19) "....is Takeshima since a long time ago called Isotake(磯竹島). It is a thickly wooded large island. From here looking toward Korea, is closer than looking at Unshū from Onshū,...."
(…竹島あり、古より是を磯竹嶋と云う。竹木繁茂して大島の由、是より朝鮮を望めば隠州より雲州を見るより尚近し…), *Onshū Shichō Gōki*, Tagawa Kōcho, p.41; "見高麗猶雲州望隠州，一日磯竹島"(日本輿地路程全図, Tagawa Kōcho, p.42)

jective investigation, Tagawa's view stating that of all the 州 appearing in *Onshū Shichō Gōki*, only the instances mentioned above should be read as meaning 島(an island), is not conducive to the debate.

Shimojō Masao criticizes Shin Yong−ha and Lee Han−gi saying they misread the texts because they either "ignore the most important parts" or "only quote those parts of *Onshū Shichō Gōki* suiting their argument" and "have not read all of Kokudaiki(Shimojō Masao, 2004)." His criticisms refer to them "analyzing the historical materials without having read ②" (Shimojō Masao[1996], p.69) or "arguing while only quoting (1) and (7)" (Shimojō Masao[2004], p.170). However, looking at the sources Shin or Lee Han−gi have cited, and their translation into contemporary language, Shimojō's criticism does not seem justified. If one says Shin and Lee made a mistake, it is actually where Shimojō Masao says they did not cite or interpret the text being "the most important place" as a whole. This does not constitute a problem in interpreting "然則日本之乾地, 以此州爲限矣" among relevant historical materials.

For, firstly, the logic in "the most important place" does not directly have an effect on "然則日本之乾地, 以此州爲

限矣." In "the most important," a standpoint is taken that an east−west−south−north was seen from Oki omitting the words 隱岐國(隱岐島) as in 從是南(從是), 辰巳, (從是)未申, (從是)自子至卯 and (從是)戌亥間. If one says the meaning or logic of "taking 隱岐 as the point of reference" affects the whole of the last phrase "然則日本之乾地, 以此州爲限矣," then there is no need to change the grammatical subject of the sentence. Since the subject of the sentence was changed from designating Oki as the starting point, to designating Japan as the starting point, the phrase *Inui no Chi*(乾地)[north−western border of Japan] was intentionally written. [20]

Secondly, Tagawa Kōcho also left out "the most important place" when he interpreted the historical document. What Tagawa needed in order to interpret the last phrase "然則日本之乾地, 以此州爲限矣" was only the part below this phrase; "If one travels two days and one night in

---

20) It would be inadequate to say Oki Islands is in the north−west of Japan because of the statement "if one makes Edo(Tokyo) the centre, Oki Islands will be in the west"(Shimojō Masao 1996, p.70). From the standpoint of the Edo period, since one goes to 伯耆國 米子 in the west of Edo[or Kyoto] (or one goes westerly to 播磨國 姬路 and then goes again to 伯耆國 米子 in the north−west), it is natural to think that Oki lay in the north−west. In addition, if one says something is in the west when looked at from Edo, this would indicate Nagasaki(長崎). Even after considering the example of Nagasaki, Okishima should be placed in the northwest.

north-westerly direction there is Matsushima." (戌亥の間、行くこと二日一夜にして松島あり). Such selective quoting is essentially what also Shin Yong-ha and Lee Han-gi have done.

Tagawa only selected and interpreted the phrase "見高麗如自雲州望隱岐, 然則日本之乾地以此州爲限矣," and Shimojō Masao is merely following in his steps. As mentioned before not only is there no mention of Takeshima(Ulleungdo) being under Japanese jurisdiction in the phrase "見高麗如自雲州望隱岐," but if read carefully there are also no such comments in the whole of *Onshū Shichō Gōki*. Nevertheless, the phrase "seeing Goryeo is the same as seeing Onshū from Unshū is written based upon the understanding that the location Goryeo is seen is naturally assumed to be Japanese territory. Thus, such phrases as either "among Takeshima, Ulleungdo and Okishima, only from Ulleungdo can been seen Korea as seeing Okishima from Unshū(Shimane)," or "Among these islands(Takeshima, Ulleungdo, Okishima) there is no island, except Ulleungdo, from which it is possible to see Korea, in the same way as seeing Okishima from Unshū(Shimane) (Shimojō Masao 1996, p.96) resulted from the mistaken belief that Takeshima(Ulleungdo) was marked as Japanese. Ulleungdo is the only Japanese territory, mentioned in *Kokudaiki*, from which Goryeo can been seen, resulted from the mistaken belief that Takeshima(Ulleungdo) was marked as Japanese.

Shimojō Masao(2004, p.171) states that "the only place mentioned in *Kokudaiki* from which it is possible to see Goryo from Japanese territory, is Ulleungdo." It is a mistake to claim the text states that Takeshima(Ulleungdo) is Japanese territory.

Shimojō Masao(2004, p.171) states that in Izumohan, there was a reason for why Takeshima(Ulleungdo) had been mistaken for Japanese territory at the time of *Onshū Shichō Gōki* being written. The main reason for this misunderstanding can be found where *Onshū Shichō Gōki* repeatedly mentions that Yonago's Ooya and Murakawa families sailed to Takeshima. The main ground for this misunderstanding is sought from the fact that *Onshū Shichō Gōki* repeatedly mentions Yonago's Ooya and Murakawa families sailed to Takeshima. It is true that Yonago's Ooya and Murakawa families had received a license(竹島渡海免許) and sailed to 竹島(Ulleungdo) once a year staying there to fish for months at a time. There is the tendency to believe that because the Ooya and

Murakawa families told that they had received Takeshima (Ulleungdo) and Matsushima (Takeshima/Dokdo) from *shogun*, it therefore was under Japanese jurisdiction. However, the license(竹島渡海免許) was no more than a license to cross the sea which the Ooya and Murakawa families had received through an intermediary of the Abe (阿部) family, who were Hatamoto(旗本)[a direct vassal of *Shogun* in the Edo period], in order to eliminate other competitors. No one except the two families and their employees were allowed to sail to Takeshima(Ulleungdo). They will only have sailed out to Takeshima(Ulleungdo) once a year and because when the fishing season was over they returned to the territory of Tottorihan(鳥取藩), nobody actually lived on the island.[21] Looking at this situation objectively, one can hardly say this means it was "Japanese territory."

---

21) One cannot consider each place in Southeast Asia where people are in possession of 'a license to travel to foreign countries'(異國渡海朱印狀) Japanese territory. The simple fact that Japanese lived there and set up a village, does not make the island Japanese territory. Not to mention there is no evidence of Japanese having lived there. Even so, it is beyond imagination that land where no one lived and people would only have been able to sail to if they were employees of the Ooya and Murakawa families could have been considered Japanese territory at the time. Moreover, 竹島渡海免許and 異國渡海朱印狀 are of a different nature. The afore was only granted once in 1625, and the *Shogunate* did not keep track of sailing either(Ikeuchi Satoshi 1999). Actually, the *Shogunate* was not even fully aware that Takeshima(Ulleungdo) existed at all(Ikeuchi Satoshi 2001).

In December 1695(*Genroku* 8) and slightly later than in the period discussed above, Tottorihan of *Edohantei*(江戸藩邸) replied that: "Takeshima was not an island belonging to either Inaba(因幡) or Hoki(伯耆)" to an inquiry by the Rōjū(老中)[title used in the Edo period for an official in charge of the affairs of state under the *Shogun*'s immediate control] Masao(阿部正男). On January 9 of the following year, considering this reply, the *Shogunate* said to Rōjū of Tsushimahan such things as "one cannot say the island (Takeshima) is part of Inaba or Hoki and," "If Japanese lived there or our side acquired it, it would be difficult to give back now. Yet, there is no proof of it." ([竹島]は因幡、伯江附屬と申ニ而も無之、日本人居住候か、此方江取候島ニ候ハ、今更遣しかたき事候江共、左樣之証據等も無之) (Ikeuchi Satoshi 2001, pp.19–20). In other words, Tottorihan said it never had control of Takeshima (Ulleungdo), and the *Shogunate* also declared it never considered Ulleungdo its territory.

While the Ooya and Murakawa families were only engaging in exclusive fishing around Takeshima(Ulleungdo), the island had never been Japanese. Nor had it been understood as such.[22]

---

22) The debate, which was argued in the so-called *Genroku Takeshima Itken*(元

(3) In support of the idea that 此州 means Ulleungdo (2)

A footnote referring to Takeshima, attached to a historical document is another factor on which the author of *Onshū Shichō Gōki* based his understanding that Takeshima (Ulleungdo) was under Japanese jurisdiction. Referring to Isotake(五十猛) in 神言, this footnote explains why Takeshima was given the different name Isotakeshima(磯竹島). This description would not have been possible unless Takeshima(Ulleungdo) had been recognized as Japanese territory. However, taking [source 1] as an example, there are copies of *Onshū Shichō Gōki* where this *Ango*(按語)[an annotation added during duplication] appears and there are some where it does not (see table 2). Therefore, the above mentioned *Ango*(按語) was not present in what Saito Hōzen(齋藤豊仙) wrote and was added on later, or it was present at first but for some reason was among parts deleted later on.

祿 竹島 一件)[*Genroku*, Case Concerning Takeshima], was not on territorial sovereignty of Takeshima(Ulleungdo). What the Ooya and Murakawa families sought was a guarantee to fish the waters around Takeshima(Ulleungdo). They were not appealing to maintain Japanese jurisdiction. Entrusted with the negotiations, Tsushimahan(對馬藩) had no interest in dealing with territorial problem initially. Territorial sovereignty only became a topic in the negotiations when the Korean(then Joseon) government side demanded Japan clearly state Ulleungdo was Korea's territory(Ikeuchi Satoshi, 2001).

Table 2. Similarities and differences on Isotakeshima(磯竹島) in an inserted note and assumptions

	No 按語	With 按語		Year duplicated
		神書	神言	
續々群書類從	○			
日本庶民生活史料集成	○			
鶴舞図書館・河村文庫		○		After mid 1740s (*1)
西尾市岩瀬文庫		○		After first year of 宝暦 (1751) (*2)
Seoul National University Library			○	Second year of 享和 (1802)

*1. The fact that there is a seal of 「河 藏書」(河村秀根藏書印) indicates that this booklet is a part of books compiled by Kawamura Hidene(河村秀根). The above assumption can be made based on the fact that 秀根 lived 1719−92 and engaged in studies in his twenties from *Kokushi Daijiten*(「國史大辭典」[Dictionary of National History] by Kawamura Hidene).

*2. The phrase "南窓随筆抄 燒火權現" appears at the end of the volume, because "destroyed by fire in the third month of the first year of Hōreki (宝暦)" also appears in the records.

*3 *Hakugaki*(奧書) states that the piece was written in the second year of Kyōwa(亭和).

In relation to this, one needs to pay attention to *Okikuni Fudoki*(隱岐國風土記)[A Topography of Oki State] in *Iwanamibunko shiryō*(岩瀬文庫史料)[historic materials reserved in Iwanami Library] of Nishioshi(西尾

市)[Nishio City]. This report dating from 1709 (the 6th year of 宝永[Hōei]) was written in Oki by Kyoto's doctor Ozeki Okusen(尾關意仙) who had been banished to Oki State(隱岐國) for murder. This is known to have been sent to a doctor of Ise(伊勢: today's Mie Prefecture) in Kōbe in 1736[the first year of *Genbun*(元文)]. The report begins with the following description (source 2). When compared with (source 1) it becomes clear at a glance that it is a description derived from Kokudaiki in *Onshū Shichō Gōki*.

[Source 2]
隱州者在北海中故名隱岐嶋矣,其在選地言島前なり、凡二郡、知夫郡、海部郡村數十三屬焉、其位震地言島後、凡二郡周吉郡・穩地郡村數五十三屬焉、其府者周吉郡南岸西郷豊崎也、從是之方至出雲三保關海上三十五里、至同積積浦・北浦十八里、至長門下關百里、巽之方至伯州赤崎四十里、艮之方至若州小浜百二十里、自子至卯無可往地、乾之間二晝一夜走而有松島、又一晝走有竹嶋、俗言磯竹嶋、此二島無人之地也、或云、春夏秋之間朝鮮人來漁鮑・海鹿之類乎、寬文年中□者自隱州滯舟而漁採桐・杪檀・竹芳之類歸也、近年關其、從竹嶋見高麗如自雲州望隱州、然則日本之乾地、以此州爲限矣

Comparing the underlined phrase with the corresponding part in source 1: "戌亥間行二日一夜二有松島一、又一日程有竹島(割注)「俗言磯竹島多竹・魚・海鹿「(、按、神言所謂五十猛歟)」、此二島無レ人之地," one notices that the added 按語 part raising the issue is not present.

As an example, Oki Kokishū(隠岐古記集)[A Compilation of Old Records on Oki], completed in 1823 (source 3 quoted below), gives the following explanation for calling Takeshima Iso·take·shima(磯・竹・島) that "That island has a high mountain called Igudake(弓嵩) to its north−east. Maybe the people of the time called the island Iso·take·shima(磯・嵩・島) after said mountain (underlined phrase ウ)." In investigating the origins of the name Isotake(磯竹島), the book states "since the olden days our country(here Oki State) has called it Isotake(磯竹島) (割注)," and also cites a phrase in *Onshū Shichō Gōki* saying "being seen(視聴合記に見へらり)." However, Isotake(五十孟) was not mentioned.

Considering this, one of the following must be true. Either the 按語 relating to Isotake(五十猛) in the corresponding part of *Onshū Shichō Gōki* had not been written when *Okikuni Fudoki* and *Oki Kokishū* were completed; or the point of view had appeared in writing but the author of *Okikuni Fudoki* and *Oki Kokishū* did not use it.

If this is the case, it would not be appropriate to say the problem surrounding the part about 按語 is the position Saito Hōzen(齋藤豊仙) takes in his writings since 1667. Even if one assumes this section did exist in 1667, what is important is that people afterwards did not make use of it. In either case, it would be difficult to conclude that Takeshima(Ulleungdo) was considered Japanese territory in Oki state, based on the *Ango*(按語).

However, Naitō Seitchū also argued that it was "proper to describe Takeshima(Ulleungdo) as the north–western border of Japan," as he cited *Oki Kokishū* in saying as follows.

Oonishi Oshiyasu's(大西敎保) *Oki Kokishū* of 1823 (Bunsei 6) recorded: "Korea looks further away when looking at it from this island than when looking at Unshū from Onshū. And people from Korea have come to live on it" [此島より朝鮮を望免は隱州より雲州を見るより 猶遠して、今は朝鮮人來て住すと言ふ]. This clearly indicates '此島' is Takeshima (Ulleungdo). As it is said that this book was a new edition revised and enlarged based upon *Onshū Shichō Gōki*, the north–western limit of Japan (日本の 乾地) mentioned in *Onshū Shichō Gōki* is Takeshima(Ulleungdo).[Naitō Seichū, p.122]

First, *Oki Kokishū* listed as [source 3] is quoted below.[23] Then the first part of *Onshū Shichō Gōki · Kokudaiki* was extracted from [source 1] and was written together with [source 4] with differences between the two books being considered.

[Source 3]

隠州の所在は、歴代史を考るにa日本の乾地此國を以限りとする也、b雲州三保關ヨリ三拾五里、c震地に在る島後といふ、周吉郡、越智郡焉に屬す、其の南岸をd西郷といふ、國中の府とす、東は大久村ヨリ西は油井村迄長五里三拾町、北は西村より南は今津村迄横五里半とす、嶋の惣廻り拾八里程、e是ヨリ坤地に位するを嶋前といふ、知夫里郡・海士郡焉に屬す、所謂三つに分る（割注）「知夫里郡二嶋、海士郡壹嶋」、別府村を以府とす、其南は知夫里村より北は宇賀村・冠島之磯迄四里余長とす、東は布施村ヨリ西は美田村船越の西の出島迄三里半とす、島之惣周里拾六

---

23) *Oki Kokishū* is reprinted and inserted in this article from materials collated and published by the National Institute of Korean History(NIKH). This text is known to have been collated by Kang Man−gil in the 1970s. However, there are no records on where the materials were collected. Also, the chapter *Okishima Shiryō*(隠岐島史料)[Historical materials of Oki Islands] in 隠岐郷土研究會 has been merged with *Oki Kokishū* in the modern edition. The texts are mostly the same. However, in the *Okishima Shiryō* version "里" has been changed to '厘'. There are many slight differences which do not affect the context as such. In the modern edition there is one part differing greatly from the older version with notes appearing in [ ], there are three occasions where [イ] appears.

里程、又f未申ノ方五拾八里にして石州温泉津に至る、g辰巳ノ方四拾里伯州赤碕あり、ア卯方凡百里にして若州小浜に至り、丑寅之方凡三拾里余能州に当る、h亥ノ方四十余里にして松前^島あり、周り凡壹里程にして生木なき岩嶋といふ、i又酉ノ方七十余里余に竹嶋（あり、古より是を磯竹嶋）といひ伝ふj竹木繁茂して大島の由、k是より朝鮮を望めは隠州より雲州を見るより尚近しと云、イ今は朝鮮人往來すと云々、愚諸國の船人に問尋するに方角誠に然り、秋清天北風の日に大満寺山の頂上ヨリ望み見は、松島は遙か見へんといふ、ウ竹嶋は朝鮮の池山^{(イ)地}に懐かれ遠く望めは朝鮮地と見ゆる由、愚按、当國にて古ヨリ磯竹と云伝へあり、（割注）「視聴合記に見へたり」今や朝鮮の図面を見るに、彼國市師^{(イ)京}より寅卯ノ方、亦對馬國豊浦より子ノ方に当りて鬱陵嶋といふあり、其嶋の丑の方に弓嵩^{イグタケ}とて高山有と見ゆ、彼嵩を呼んて当地の人磯嵩嶋と号しならんか、当國に百里の内外に彼二嶋より外見へさる由なり、人の住居する近頃にてハ、有まじ

[Source 4]
隠州在二北海中一故隠岐嶋（割注）「按、倭訓海中言二遠幾一故名歟」e´其在二選地一言二島前一也、知夫郡・海部郡^{アマ}屬レ焉、c´其位二震地一言二島後一、周吉郡^{シキチ}・穏地^{ヲチ}

郡屬レ焉、d′其府者周吉郡南岸西鄕豊崎也、從レ是南
至二 b′雲州美穗關三十五里、g′辰巳至二伯州赤碕浦一四
十里、f′未申至二石州溫泉津一五十八里、自レ子至レ卯無
二可レ往地一、h′戌亥間行二日一夜有二松島一、i′又一日
程有二竹島一 (割注)「俗言二磯竹島一j′多二竹・魚・海鹿
一」、此二島無レ人之地、k′見二高麗一如下自二雲州一望中
隱岐上、然則 a′日本之乾地、以二此州一爲レ限矣、

The underlined phrases a and a' and k and k' appear
both in *Oki Kokishū* and *Onshū Shichō Gōki* · Kokudaiki,
and these sections show that the articles correspond with
each other. One can say that the not underlined part of
the text correlates with sections appearing after the second volume of *Onshū Shichō Gōki*. And because it seems
that extended knowledge based upon events between
1660s and 1820s was reflected in underlined section ア－
イ, one may conclude that *Oki Kokishū* is definitely an
extended version based on *Onshū Shichō Gōki*.[24] In this

24) In 1735 (year 20 of *Kyōho*[亨保]) a four-seater boat, belonging to 隱岐
島後, went to 越前 on business and on its way back drifted onto the
Korean peninsula. [Mazuda Kō](松田甲). This event shows that at the
beginning of the 18th century it had at least been possible to travel from
Oki and Yukasazu(若狹) and to the environs of Echizen(越前) · Noto(能
登). With broadening knowledge, the understanding of the description of
the north-eastern direction in *Onshū Shichō Gōki*, "There is no land[往
くべき地なし]," was changed and connected to the description of イ in
the sections marked with dots. In the 17th century, events of 元祿 竹島
一件 would have followed the underlined section イ.

instance one must not ignore the corresponding relation between part a: "日本の乾地此國を以て限りとする也" and a': "日本之乾之地、以二此州一爲レ限矣." Laying at the heart of the debate surrounding the interpretation of *Onshū Shichō Gōki*, the above mentioned phrases elucidate that '此州' refers to '此國(隱岐國)' and that '此州' is none other than 'Japan's 乾地'. However, when comparing *Oki Kokishū* and *Onshū Shichō Gōki* it is not in the least possible to come to Naitō's conclusion that Takeshima(Ulleungdo) is Japan's 乾地.

Conclusion

Shimojō Masao is right in saying that, "After all one doesn't just read one part of a historical text and interpret it. Shouldn't one look at the whole text?," which essentially means: "Shouldn't one read historical materials a bit more carefully?"(1996, p.70 top). He was also correct in pointing out that one cannot just "quote and interpret parts of *Onshū Shichō Gōki* that suit one's own argument and not read all of *Kokudaiki* (Shimojō Masao 2004, p.168)." This article dealt with *Onshū Shichō Gōki* in detail in order not to receive such criticism.

However, *Onshū Shichō Gōki* is not the hitherto oldest

record mentioning Takeshima/Dokdo being called Matsushima. For Takeshima/Dokdo appears under the island name of Matsushima, among documents of the Ooya family, written presumably in the early 1650s. Further to how this document does not prove that Takeshima/Dokdo was under Japanese jurisdiction in the 1660s was discussed above.

On the one hand, this document proves that Takeshima/Dokdo was outside Japanese jurisdiction at the time (presented in opinion II above), but one should not interpret this as saying "that it is Korea's territory"(II). Therefore, using *Onshū Shichō Gōki* to uncover historical proof of whom Takeshima/Dokdo must be returned to, is not advisable for either the Japanese or the Korean side. First of all it is necessary to distance oneself from such a debate.

* In the original this article includes a note: (「隱州視聽合紀 (記)」に言及した諸論考), which has been omitted[here]. Please consult the attached original about this section. [added by the translator]

[Original 『青丘學術論集』 25 (2001.3), pp. 147−184]

Ahn Yong—bok in Oki(隱岐)

Naitō Seichū(內藤正中)[1]

1. Introduction

Ahn Yong—bok is the one person who must be mentioned in connection with Japan and Korea's confrontation over the sovereignty of Takeshima(Dokdo). It is said that Ahn, who was from Dongrae, Gyeongsang Province of Korea, came to Hoki(伯耆) State[伯耆國: the eastern part of present—day Tottori Prefecture, also mentioned as Hokishū (州)] in Japan in the 17th century, and received written

[1] Professor emeritus at Shimane University, former chief of the Northeast Culture Research Center at Tottori College and visiting professor at the same university.

confirmation(書契) that Ulleungdo and Jasando(Dokdo) were Korean territory from the Lord of Tottorihan (western part of present−day Tottori Prefecture). He is a special feature in Korean middle and high school history textbooks on the basis that he is the individual who claimed Korean sovereignty over Dokdo against Japan.

The fact that Ahn Yong−bok claimed Korean sovereignty of Dokdo in Japan was recorded in *Joseon Wangjo Sillok*(朝鮮王朝實錄)[Annals of the Joseon[2] Dynasty] and other records.] However, such documents are only based on his testimony made when he was seized and underwent questioning by the *Bibyeonsa*(備邊司)[Office of Border Defense] after returning from Hoki state. There are no historical documents objectively establishing his testimony as authentic. One can say that it is problematic that the records merely state that the others captured with Ahn gave the same description. Since this incident took place first of all in Japan, there is a need to compare records with the Japanese side, especially with Tottorihan as the other party concerned. Fortunately, as there are historical materials by the Ikeda family(池田家) including

---

2) Joseon is a name for Korea. Korea was named Joseon during the Joseon Dynasty(1392−1910).

for example *Inpu Nenppyō*(因府年表) or *Takeshimakō*(竹島考) in Tottorihan relating to this incident, we can find out about Ahn Yong−bok's words and actions in both countries Hoki(伯耆) and Inaba(因幡), and about how the Tottorihan dealt with the situation. I have introduced and analyzed materials on Ahn Yong−bok in the two countries Inho(因伯)[Inaba and Hoki State] in *Takeshima o Meguru Nitchō Kankeishi*(竹島[獨島] を めぐる日朝關係史)[History of Japanese−Korean Relations Concerning Takeshima](Taga Publishing, 2000).

Records of Ahn Yong−bok's interrogation when he arrived in Hoki State in May 1696(Genroku 9) were discovered in May 2005 in Shimane Prefecture's Oki County in Amachō(島根縣隱岐郡海士町) in the Murakami(村上) household.

The document's title is *Genroku Kyūsonoeumatoshi Chōsenbune Hyōchaku Itkan no Oboegaki*(元祿九丙午年朝鮮舟漂着一卷之覺書). As Oki Island came under Matsuehan's jurisdiction in 1721, the *Oojōya* system(大庄屋制) was introduced with the Murakami family becoming *Oojōya* representing two of Dōzen's counties. Although Oki State(present−day Oki Island) had remained under the jurisdiction of Matsuehan between 1638 and 1687, it was a dominion of the *Shogunate* between 1688 and 1720, and came under the jurisdiction of Oomori Daikan(代官)[a local official who governs dominions of the *Shogunate*] of Ginzanryō of Iwamikuni[石見國:present−day western part of Shimane Prefecture]. Therefore, because the number of *Jaiban Yakunin*(在藩役人)[high−ranking officials in a Han] dispatched to Oki from the *Daikanshō*(代官所) was small, the Oojōya was put in charge of everyday administrative affairs. I think this is how the family came to witness the incoming Korean ship being investigated, and the records came to be passed down.

There were 11 people, including Ahn Yong−bok, aboard the Korean ship that arrived on the Nishimura(西村) coast of Dōgo(島後), Oki State on 18 May, 1696 (*Genroku* 9). While being interrogated Ahn presented *Paldo Chongdo*(朝鮮八道地圖)[Map of Eight Provinces of Korea] and made it clear that the islands called Takeshima and Matsushima in Japan belonged to Korea's Gangwon Province. They also remarked that they had stopped here on their way to submit a petition(訴願) to the Lord of Hokishū(伯耆守), and that they were waiting for a fair wind to cross the sea to Hakushū(伯州).

Ahn Yong-bok's party crossed over to Akasaki(赤崎) in Hoki State on June 6. On May 23, Oki State submitted a repot written in the style of a memorandum to *Onyakusho*(御役所: a government office) in Sekishū(石州) of Oomori. For this reason, we cannot know the circumstances of their stay between May 22 and June 4. Tottorihan records inform us in detail about their stay in Tottorihan up until June 21, when they entered Tottorihan's *Jōka*(城下)[the settlement formed around a castle]. Records of their 50 day stay there until August 6 are presented in an edited and concise form, possibly in order to avoid rumors spreading.

For that reason there are no historical materials on the Tottorihan side that could confirm wether or not Ahn Yong-bok's claim of meeting and telling the Lord of Tottorihan that Takeshima and Matsushima are Korea's Ulleungdo and Jasando is true. However, from *Chōsen Bune Chakugan Itkan no Oboegaki*(朝鮮舟着岸一卷之覺書) researched by *Daikansho Yakunin*(代官所 役人)[an official of Daikansho] of Oki, we can confirm that Ahn had come with the purpose of going to Hoki State(伯耆州), and had prepared to claim Takeshima and Matsushima as Korean territory. Further, when he arrived in Hoki, a banner was draped across the bow of the ship bearing the words 朝鬱兩島監稅將臣安同知騎 written with a brush. This can be understood as showing his intentions to raise the territorial claims he mentioned in Oki earlier. For various reasons such as this, the testimonies Ahn made at *Bibyeonsa* are simply being disclaimed as fabrications. I think it is necessary to reexamine them.

Matsushima(present−day Takeshima/Dokdo[獨島]) was called Usando during the Joseon Dynasty, but Ahn Yong−bok used the name Jasando(子山島) in his statement to *Bibyeonsa*, and when he was in Oki. Therefore, this paper will use Jasando.

2. A Ship from Korea arrives in Oki

The Korean ship arrived in Nishimura(西村) in Dōgo(島後), Oki on May 18, 1696(*Genroku* 9). However, because of the strong swell there, it moved on to Nakamura(中村), and on the evening of the 19th entered Ookumura's(大久村) Kayoi(かよい) haven. On the 20th it was investigated by a *Jaihan Yakunin*(在藩役人)[an official in the Han] who rushed in from Saigo(西鄉). The investigation finished on the 22nd and when the *Saihan Yakunin* wrote the report that was to be presented to Yakusho(役所)[a government office], Ahn's party was about to be ordered back to Saigo. But, due to heavy rain and strong winds they stayed in Ookumura.

The ship was 9m long(3丈), 3.6m wide(2尺), 1.3m deep(4尺 and 2寸), could seat 80 stones(80石), and was equipped with two masts(帆檣), two sails(帆), a rudder (梶), five oars(櫓) and two anchors(木碇). Apart from bearing two cotton banners(幟), four bundles of paper mulberry(楮), matting to spread underneath and dog's leather were attached to the ship's prow.

These items were also listed under the title *Chōsen Bune ni Korearu Dōgu no Oboe*(朝鮮船在之道具之覺). It lists white rice (about three Hop[540ml] remaining in a bag), three *Hyō*(表) of kelp, one *Hyō* of salt, a sack of dried abalone, a bundle of firewood six *Shaku*(尺) eight *Sun*(寸) long, one *Shaku* round, six bamboo poles, three *Shaku* five *Sun* long, three *Shaku* round, a knife (crude and cannot be used as a weapon), *Yōshi*(要指)[a kind of waist knife−even though stated as being for self−protection, it is a knife for cooking or to eat with], four spears(鑓)[all said to be used to catch abalone, the longest about four 尺], a long knife(長刀), a small bow(半弓), a box of arrows, two masts[one of them eight 尋(about

12m)], the other six 尋(about 9m, one made of bamboo), a rudder(梶)[one 丈 four 尺 five 寸], about 10 shades made of straw(王綱)(two of them are five 尺, one 丈 two 尺 wide, the remaining slightly larger than those in Japan), three sheets(枚) of dog's leather, three mats(枚) to spread out on the floor, etc. The list also reads "noted exactly as was found during examination(右之通見分仕候處粉無御座候)."

There were 11 people on the ship. Only five names were taken down: Ahn Yong-bok(安龍福), Lee Bi-won(李裨元), Kim Ga-gwa(金可果), Noe Heon(雷憲) and Yeon Seup(衍習). Only Ahn Yong-bok, Noe Heon and Yeon Seup were listed with their ages. The other three civilians' and three (buddhist) monks' ages and names are not mentioned.

Ahn Yong-bok was described as 43 years old, wearing a *Gat*(a traditional Korean hat) that resembled *Gwan*(冠)[a crown], a string of crystals(緒) and an identity tag(札) with the words: *Tongjeongdaebu*(通政大夫)[an official during the Joseon Dynasty], born in Gapo(甲午)[43 years old], a *Judongrae*(住東萊)[live in Dongrae] engraved on it. Attached to his fan was a small box containing his seal(印判) and another box for a pipestem for the ears.

Kim Ga−gwa is also described as wearing a black *Gat*[a traditional Korean hat] similar to a crown and a fine cotton jacket woven with white yarn. He did not have a fan, and his age was unknown.

Noe Heon was the head priest of Heung Wang Temple (興旺寺), 55 years old, wore a black *Gat* similar to a crown, was wearing a fine beautifully woven coat, and was holding a fan. He had a document dated *Ganghee*(康熙) 8th year, March 20 bearing a red seal of Keumosan (金烏山), and a case one 尺 long, four 寸 wide and four 寸 high. In a case with a locking device there was a bamboo Sangi(算木)[a tool for calculating], an ink slab(硯), and a brush and ink. Also, there were about 10 prayer beads similar to those used in Japan.

Yeon Seup was described as Noe Heon's 33 year old apprentice monk. His attire matched that of Noe Heon. The other three monks said they had joined the party to have a look at Takeshima.

As a result of the above examination, the names, ages, clothing and items brought along were surveyed. The following table shows that names of ten people, excluding Noe Heon, had changed everytime they were interrogated.

Ahn Yong-bok in Oki(隠岐)

'Hoki' in the table refers to the investigation by the Tottorihan officials who came to Hoki by ship. It is based upon the record entitled *Takeshimakō*(竹島考). The column 'after returning to their country' are details the *Bibyeonsa* collected in *Joseon Wangjo Sillok*(朝鮮王朝實錄)[Records of the Joseon Dynasty].

Oki(隱岐)	Hoki(伯耆)	after returning to their country
Ahn Yong-bok aged 43	Ahn Dong-ji (朝鬱兩島監稅將)	Ahn Yong-bok (from Dongnae)
Lee Bi-won	Kim Bi-jang (進士軍官)	Lee In-seong (from Pyeongsanpo)
Kim Ga-gwa	Kim Bi-jang (進士軍官)	Kim Seong-gil (From Nakan)
Kim I-gwan	Kim Sa-gong (帶率)	
Yu Sang-gong	Yu Gak-sol (帶率)	Yu Il-bu (from Heunghae)
Yuukai	Yu Han-bu (帶率)	Yu Bong-seok (from Yeonghae)
Noeheon aged 55	Noeheon (金烏僧將 釋氏)	Noeheon (a monk from Sunch'eon)
Yeonseup aged 33	Seuphwaju (釋氏帶率僧)	Kim Sun-rip (from Chaekyeonan)
Yeongyul	Yulhwaju (釋氏帶率僧)	Yeongyuldan (Seungdam yeonseup)

Seungdam	Dambeopju (釋氏帶率僧)	
Dancheak	Chaekhwaju (釋氏帶率僧)	
朝鮮舟着岸一卷之覺書	竹島考	朝鮮王朝實錄

The interrogation took place with Ahn Yong−bok, Noe Heon and Kim Ga−gwa acting as representatives and answering the investigator's(在藩役人) questions for the other eight persons. At the time it was recorded that Ahn Yong−bok, "answered the questions as a translator(通祠ニテ事ヲ問申候得バ, 答申候)." This means that he translated his questions and answers into Japanese. It is said that Ahn learnt Japanese from frequently visiting the Japanese residence(倭館) in Busan. He called himself a Japanese interpreter(和語通詞) when he was taken from Takeshima and brought to Yonaga in 1693(*Genroku* 6). Nevertheless, after conversing with confucian scholars in Aoya's(靑谷) Senenji(專念寺) in Hoki State, Ahn Yong−bok had once said he could not speak Japanese, until he entered Tottori Castle's *Jōka* (城下).

3. Ahn Yong-bok in *Genroku* 6

When the *Jaihan Yakunin* interrogated him Ahn Yong−bok said that, "four years ago in the summer of 酉年(1693) I was seized by a ship from Hakushū(伯州) and brought here (四年己前酉夏竹島二而伯州之丹二被連まいり 候)." This means that four years earlier he had been taken to Hoki from Takeshima. He added that at the time he had been together with a man called Toribe(朴於屯), and that this time he had left him on Takeshima.

Four years before 1696(*Genroku* 9) is 1692, but 酉年 corresponds to 1693. In March of that year, two people called Ahn Pingshya(Ahn Yong−bok referred to as 安兵使 read with Japanese pronunciation) and Torahe(朴於屯) had been seized on Takeshima and taken to Yonago. The Japanese side's records referring to that time note the following.

In 1692(*Genroku* 5) Murakawa's ship arrived on Takeshima and they met Koreans for the first time. However, taken aback by the large number of some 53 Koreans, because they were only 21 people on the Japanese side, they took some items to prove that Korean people were there, and hurried back. Because there was someone who spoke Japanese among the Koreans, the Japanese sternly asked, "We received this island from the *Shogunate*'s general and sail here every year. Why is it that you are here? (此島之義公方樣より拝領仕り, 毎年渡海いたし候島にて候ところに、何として参り候や)." This was recorded by the ship's captain in Kōjð no Oboe (口上之覺).

In March of 1693 the Ooya family's ship sailed out again. That year also, people from Korea were there, and because the same interpreter they met the year before was there they took him aboard and sailed back. The Japanese took him to Yonago to sternly tell him not to return to the island again, since the people from Korea had returned despite the (Japanese) warning not to return to Takeshima under any circumstances.

Two Korean people were taken and left Takeshima on March 18. They arrived in Fukuura(福浦), Oki on the 20th and were interrogated by *Jaihan Yakunin*. On the 23rd, about the time when they left Fukuura, the captain gave the two Koreans a cask of an alcoholic drink, but it is not known why.

The Ooya's ship arrived back in Yonago on the 27th

by way of Dōzen, and the two men were held at the house of Ooya Kyūemon(大谷九右衛門) in Nadachō(灘町). Tottorihan arranged for two low−ranking warriors to watch and guard them. Ara Ookatsu(荒尾大和) and his uncle Arao Shuri(荒尾修理) were dispatched from Tottori and placed in charge of the interrogation. One month later, on April 28 Koreans' *Kōsho*(口書)[transcript of testimony] and three bundles of documents Koreans in possession of(唐人の口書、並に所持候書三通) were sent to the Tottorihan office. On the 30th, the report was sent on to the *Hantei*(藩邸)[Han's office] in Edo(江戸).

After the questioning, among the pages in the *Hikaechō*(控帳)[a record book] of Tottorihan written while waiting for instructions from Edo, there is a note on May 11 referring to Ahn Yong−bok saying that, "Shyuri(荒尾修理) heard that Ahn Ping−shya(the Japanese interpreter) said he wanted to go outside to lift his spirits. However, Shyuri ordered not to let him go outside. [Ahn] also wanted to drink alcohol. Likewise [the Shyuri] said no more than three Shō(升) a day were permitted. (アンビンシュン（和語通詞なり）氣晴に出可申、色"Xわやく申候由、修理迄申來候得共、外に出候事無用と差図申事、且又酒給申度候得共、是又晝夜に

三升より上は無用の由、申達候事)." If that was May 11, and they were seized and taken to Yonago for questioning on March 27, then almost 50 days had passed. After the investigation was over and Ahn Yong−bok had submitted his *Kōsho*(口書) again, it seems that he complained about various other things apart from demanding to be able to go outside to 'lift his spirit'. Although he was not permitted to go outside, he was allowed to drink up to three *Shō* of alcoholic drinks.

The following will make clear that Ahn Ping−shya(the Japanese pronunciation for 安兵使) was interpreting the Japanese. *Takeshimakō*(竹島考) written by Okajima Masayoshi(岡嶋正義), the *Hanshi*(藩士)[an offcial of a *Han*] of Tottorihan states in 1828(*Bunsei*[文政] 11) that when (the Japanese) encountered (Ahn Yong−bok) on Takeshima, they asked his name. Its says he answered, "I live in Korea, Gyeongsang Province in Dongrae Town. I am Ahn Pingshya and am 42 years old. This person is from Ulsan, is called Torahe and is 34 years old (吾在所ハ朝鮮國慶尚道東萊縣ノ者ニテ、アンピンシャ、年齢四十二オナリ、是ナル者ハ蔚山ノ人ニテ、トラヘト云ヘリ、年齢ハ三十四オナリ)."

Ahn Yong-bok in Oki(隠岐)

The *Shogunate*'s orders were issued on May 26. The order to take the Koreans overland to Nagasaki are recorded in *Takeshimakō* as follows: "The *Shoguante*'s 老中[a high-ranking official of the *Shogunate* under a *Shogun*'s immediate control] received the *Shogun*'s order to instruct the Korean people not to sail to Takeshima again, and that he had decided to send them back to Nagasaki　(關東ノ御沙汰を歴テ、政老中ヨリ朝鮮人ヘハ、以來竹島ヘ渡海致サザル様ニ急度申含メ、肥前國長崎マデ送還スベキ旨御裁定ナリ)."

According to *Hikaechō*(控帳), the Tottorihan office had ordered that the Korean men be brought to Tottori before being sent to Nagasaki. So, they were sent from Yonago to Tottori escorted by three Samurai and a doctor. They entered Tottori Castle on June 1 and were first accommodated at 家老[patriarch] Arao Ookatsu's(荒尾大和) residence, then at the castle settlement's main hall(會所) for a week. Four senior officials came especially to meet the men from Korea on the evening of the day they were moved from Arao's house to the settlement's main hall. It is possible that they came out of curiosity. *Takeshimakō* reads that "Ahn Ping-shya had a coarse and violent personality(アンピンシャは猛性狂暴ナル者)." *Inpu Nenpyō*

(因府年表) states that "among those in the party there is fiendish person(異客の內に暴惡の者これ有る由)." Maybe because of this the Tottori issued a public announcement that "no women or children were allowed outside(女童出で候事無用)" when Ahn Yong-bok entered the *Jōka*.

When he was sent to Nagasaki they went overland, because the sea route was dangerous. We can see that the Tottorihan went to great lengths of care ordering that "each Yakunin must be prepared for anything that could happen (萬"X共御用意、夫"X役人江申渡候事)." Tottorihan appointed two vassal envoys, and sent with them a doctor, five 御徒[low-ranking warriors who could not present before a general, nor ride a horse without permission], some low-ranking soldiers(輕卒), 御小人[in charge of any chores], a 飛脚[person conveying documents], and even a cook.

The party left Tottori on June 7 and arrived in Nagasaki on the 30th of the same month. On July 1, the men from Korea were handed over at 奉行所. In Nagasaki, the *Rusuiyaku*(留守居役)[mostly in charge of affairs when the lord was away] of the Tsushimahan took charge of them, and questioned them. On August 14, they

Ahn Yong-bok in Oki(隱岐)

were transferred into the hands of a guide sent from Tsushimahan and arrived in Tsushima on September 3. Ahn and his party left around the end of September and the guide led them back to Korea.

Tsushimahan's *Chōsen Tsūkō Daiki*(朝鮮通交大紀) shows that, "in *Genroku* 6 (癸酉), 40 people from Korea came to Takeshima in our Inaba State to catch fish. This year, an order was issued to send the two people caught back to their country. In September the Lord of the *Han* sent a letter on the matter to Tada Yojaemon(多田与佐衛門)." Significant is the statement "our Inabashū Takeshima (我因幡州竹島)."

Among other historical materials on the Korean side refer-ring to this is *Joseon Wangjo Sillok*. Here I will look at the following in Shin Yong−ha's *Sajeok Haeseok Dokdo* (Takeshima)[Historical Interpretation of Dokdo].

> The Japanese fishermen exceeded [the Koreans] in number. They suggested talking in depth and persuaded the [inofficial] leaders Ahn Yong−bok, Park Oe−dun and others from Ulsan, Korea to come to Oki. But they were taken to the Lord of Hokihan. Before the Lord of Oki Islands, Ahn Yong−bok insisted that Ulleungdo was Korean territory. Then he protested asking why

they had kidnapped him, since he was merely a Korea citizen going to land belonging to his own country. The Chief of Oki Islands turned Ahn over to his superior, the Lord of Hokihan. There as well, Ahn Yong-bok asserted that it was Korean territory. Further, he demanded that Japan prohibit Japanese fishermen from crossing over the border and fishing. Because the then Lord of Hokihan knew that Ulleungdo was Korean territory, he sent Ahn to *Shogunate* in Edo.

After hearing Ahn's case *Shogunate* found that his claims were consistent and acknowledged his account as truthful. The *Shogunate* made the Lord of Hokihan write a diplomatic document stating that Ulleungdo was not Japanese territory, and intended to return Ahn Yong-bok to Korea from Edo via Nagasaki and Tsushima.

However, when Ahn arrived in Nagasaki the Lord of Tsushima arrested them, and took them to Tsushima. There the document stating that Ulleungdo was not Japanese territory was taken away and they were interrogated as trespassers on Ulleungdo, Japanese territory. In addition, Tsushima returned Ahn to Dongrae, Korea, adding illegal demands toward Korea.

The historical materials on the Japanese side give priority to how they dealt with Ahn Yong-bok, who was confined in the prefecture, and to the order of how they sent him back via Yonago, Tottori, Nagasaki. In this point, the Korean historical materials were written based upon Ahn's testimony given at the *Bibyeonsa*. They are very different from the Japanese records.

Let us address the problem first. The question is wether Ahn Yong−bok had asserted that Ulleungdo was Korean territory before the Lord of Oki Island, and whether had he protested that being kidnapped and interrogated was improper. As we do not know the contents of the inter-rogation, we are left contemplating the meaning of what the captain wrote in *Kōsho*: "The *Hansho*(藩所)[Han's of-fice] sent the two men from Korea a cask of alcoholic drink." Does this not include an apology for being drag-ged away against their will?

The second point at issue is that Oki State remained under the *Shogunate*'s direct control, unconnected to Hoki State. Therefore, the *Yakunin* of Oki did not take Ahn Yong−bok over to Tottorihan. The reason why the Koreans were taken to Yonago from Oki was that the captain of the Ooya's ship wanted to complain about the seafaring enterprise being obstructed by Korean people, and Ahn Yong−bok and the others served to attest to these goings−on.

Third, the place Ahn and the others were confined to in Yonago was the Ooya residence, and Tottorihan had two *Asigaru*(足輕)[*Hosō*(步卒): foot soldiers, not Samurai] escortiong them. The *Karō*(家老)[patriarch] of Tottorihan, Arao Ookatsu and his uncle were in charge of the interrogation. One cannot confirm whether Ahn really asserted that Takeshima(Ulleungdo) was Korean territory. Neither can one deny the possibility that he did mention it. Among *Chōsho*(調書)[records] is a document which was sent to the Tottorihan office and all the way to Edo, namely Ahn Yong−bok's testimony entitled *Tōnin no Kōshō*(唐人ノ口書)[A Document of what the Foreign Man Said]. The contents of *Tōnino Kōshō* is not known. However, with the document being presented to the *Shogunate*, it becomes clear that the *Shogunate* was aware of their territorial rights to Takeshima. Thus the *Shogunate* demanded that the Korean government(then the Joseon government) prohibit its people from sailing to Takeshima. Therefore, one cannot deny that there were demands, *albeit* the particulars of these demands are unknown.

Ahn Yong-bok in Oki(隠岐)

Of course, the account of Ahn being sent from Tottori to Edo, and the *Shogunate* granting a hearing and the Lord of Tottori giving him a document stating that Ulleungdo was Korean territory, was all fabricated by Ahn himself.

The fourth point of issue is that he was dealt with completely differently and treated as a criminal. *Joseon Wangjo Sillok* reads "the silver coin and document were taken away in Tsushima(伯耆州所給銀貨及文書馬島人劫)." It says that Tsushimahan confiscated the silver coin and document received from the Lord of Tottori han, but this is not true.

Oki, Yonaga and Tottori certainly treated Ahn courteously. On the other hand, Tsushimahan, following the *Shogunate*'s demands for a ban on Koreans sailing to Takeshima, treated Ahn Yong−bok's party as criminals who had transgressed the border.

4. Ahn Yong-bok in *Genroku* 9

In 1694(*Genroku* 7) on their way to Takeshima, Murakawa and Ooya had to turn back due to severe weather conditions.

In November that same year, Murakawa(村川) and Ooya(大谷) both applied for a loan from Tottorihan, as they had done the year before, to prepare the following spring's sea crossing. At the same time, they asked what they should be done should they encounter Koreans on Takeshima. Unlike in the past, this time Tottorihan's reply was harsh. It said, "As you are frequently asking for loans, [we] cannot approve it. [You] are sailing out arbitrarily for your business. Therefore, should there be any Koreans on the island, [we] cannot issue instructions on how to deal with them (費用借用の儀渡々なるを似て、之を許可せず、渡海の事は商賣の勝手たる可く、朝鮮人在島の節の處置は差図に及難)."

Just then, the Japanese−Korean diplomatic negotiations on the "Case Concerning Takeshima(竹島一件)" began and ensued over a period of one year. At that time the Korean side stopped using the compromising expressions "our land Ulleungdo(弊境之欝陵島)" and "your land Takeshima(貴界竹島)," which sounded as if two different islands were meant. Korea put forward their claim and said "what you Japanese call Takeshisma is nothing but our country's Ulleungdo(倭人所謂竹島 即我國欝陵島)," and demanded that Japan concede. In such circumstances

Tottorihan will have reconsidered seafaring enterprise to Takeshima. Then in late 1695(*Genroku* 8) the Japanese side confirmed that Ulleungdo was Korean territory, and aiming at putting an end to the 'Takeshima affair', the *Shogunate* issued an order banning sailing to Takeshima.

It was on May 18, 1696 that Ahn Yong−bok and 10 others arrived in Oki. Because the *Shogunate*'s ban on crossing the sea had already been effected in January, there should not have been any Japanese sailing to Takeshima. However, *Joseon Wangjo Sillok* Muinjo of Sukjong 22 September, which recorded Ahn Yong−bok's testimony at the *Bibyeonsa* after his return, shows a completely different set of circumstances. Let us quote Shin Yong−ha's work.

> There was already a Japanese ship anchored at Ulleungdo. So, Ahn Yong−bok scolded them. Ulleungdo is our land by nature, why did the Japanese venture across the border?
>
> The Japanese replied the following: "We are original inhabitants of Matsushima(Usando: Jasando[于山島: 子山島]) we came upon this place by chance following fish, and are considering leaving soon."
>
> To this Ahn Yong−bok replied that "as Matsushima

is Jasando, it also is our land. How come you are living on Matsushima?". Then, the next day he went to Jasando, and found the same fishermen boiling fish in a pot. He chased them away waving a stick. They all boarded a ship and returned to Japan.

Ahn Yong−bok's party pursued them to Japan and landed at Oki Islands in Japan. The Lord of Oki Islands asked why Ahn had sailed there, and Ahn shouted in rage, "A few years ago, when I came to this place, it was agreed upon that Ulleungdo, Jasando and the other islands are Korean territory, and [I] even received a letter from the Shogun. Why is Japan rashly encroaching upon our territory?".

The Lord of Oki promised that he would definitely report Ahn's objections to Hoki State(伯耆州). However, no matter how long Ahn waited there was no news[from Hoki State]. Indignant about this Ahn put out a boat and headed for Hoki.

It has already been pointed out that Ahn Yong−bok's account of meeting Japanese people on Ulleungdo, is not a historical fact. Moreover, could he really have gone to Oki and asserted that Ulleungdo and Jasando were Korean territory? Let us look at the *Kakusho*(覺書) in the Murakami family's document.

Ahn Yong-bok in Oki(隱岐)

Ahn Yong−bok showed *Joseon Paldo Chongdo*(朝鮮八
道總圖)[Map of the Eight Provinces of Korea] to the
Jaihan Yakunin interrogating him. And he said the following about Takeshima and Matsushima.

> According to Ahn Yong−bok, Takeshima is a Bamboo
> Island(竹島). Among the islands belonging to Dongrae,
> Gangwon Province in Korea there is an island called
> Ulleungdo. [People] call it Daeseom(Bamboo Island: 竹
> 島). This is written on the 'Map of Eight Provinces of
> Korea' that Ahn possesses.
>
> Among the above islands, Matsushima is called
> Jasando. People say that it is also called Matsushima,
> and this is also recorded on the 'Map of Eight
> Provinces of Korea'.

> (安龍福が申すは、竹島は竹島と申候、朝鮮國江
> 原道東萊府の内に鬱陵島と申島があり、是を竹の
> 島と申、即八道之図に此れを記して所持仕り候
> 松島は右島の内、子山と申す島御座候、是を松
> 島と申由、是も八道之図に記し申し候)

Even though he had not been asked, Ahn Yong−bok
was stating that Takeshima was Ulleungdo, and that
Matsushima was Jasando. Moreover, he was saying that
the two islands both belong to Dongrae in Gangwon

Province, and that this is also recorded on the 'Map of Eight Provinces of Korea'. It does say that the document is included, but it is not to be found in the Murakami family text.

On the page representing the eight provinces of Korea, Takeshima and Matsushima were written in the section on Gangwon Province. That is to say, because it says 'Takeshima and Matsushima are in this province(道) [Gangwon Province](此道中二竹島松島有之),' and seeing that there are no recordings on other provinces, it appears as if it was made specifically to assert that Takeshima and Matsushima were Korean territory.

In relation to Takeshima and Matsushima's positioning, the same *Kakusho* reads as follows.

He says that he boarded a ship and left Korea after eating breakfast on March of this year, and arrived on Takeshima that evening and ate dinner.

On the March 15 [he] left Takeshima and arrived on Matsushima that same day. On the 16th of the same month he departed from Matsushima, and arrived at the Nishimura coast in Oki Island on the morning of the 18.

[He] says that the distance from Takehima to Korea is 30 *ri*, and from Takeshima to Matsushima 50 *ri*.

Ahn Yong-bok in Oki(隠岐)

(當子三月十八日、朝鮮國朝食後に出船、竹島へは夕方着、夕食を食べ申し候由、
五月十五日竹島出船、同日松島着、同十六日松島を出て、十八日朝隱岐島の內西村の磯へ着
竹島と朝鮮の間三十里、竹島と松島の間五十里これあり申し候)

The distance between Korean Uljin and Ulleungdo is 140km. The distance between Ulleungdo and present−day Takeshima(Matsushima[松島], Jasando[子山島], Dokdo[獨島]) is 92 km. Therefore, the distances given here as 30 *ri* from the Korean mainland to Takeshima and 50 *ri* from Takeshima to Matsushima, are not precise. Also, arriving on Ulleungdo in the evening after having left Korea in the morning after breakfast, was probably said with [Ahn's] statement in mind that the distance from the Korean mainland to Takeshima was 30 *ri*. Either way, such expressions serve to state Ulleungdo's proximity to Korea, thereby implying the island is Korean. Further, regarding the time frame of crossing the sea, Ahn Yong−bok said that if one departs from Takeshima on May 15, one arrives in Matsushima on the same day. If one departs from Matsushima on May 16, one arrives in Oki by the morning of 18th. This is a correct description. Saito Hōzen's book *Onshū Shichō Gōki*(隱州視聽合

紀)[Records on Observations in Oki Province] compiled in 1667(*Kanbun* 7) also records that if one travels in a north−westerly direction from Oki for two days and one night, one reaches Matsushima. Travelling another day will bring one to Takeshima.

As seen above, knowledge of where Takeshima (Ulleungdo) and Matsushima(Jasando) were positioned was exact, and the 'Map of Eight Provinces of Korea' was used to explain that both islands belong to Dongnae in Gangwon Province, Korea. The Murakami family's text *Genroku Kyūsonoeuma Chōsenbune Chakugan Itkan no Oboegaki*(元禄九丙午年朝鮮舟着岸一券之覺書) sheds light on the fact that the *Jaihan Yakunin* in Oki State on the Japanese side recorded these facts.

5. Ahn Yong-bok in Oki

Ahn Yong−bok had come all the way to Oki and made it quite clear that Takeshima(actually Ulleungdo) and Matsushima(actually Jasando) are Korean territory, consequently making the *Yakunin* record all these facts. This episode constitutes the significance of Ahn's role in this dispute over territorial rights. Among Japanese documents, only the Murakami family's document *Kakusho*(覺

書) recorded this fact. It can not be found in Tottorihan documents. Therefore, one must conclude that the only historical source confirming the historical fact that Ahn had claimed that Jasando(Dokdo) belonged to Korea before the Japanese is said *Kakusho*, which recorded his comments and actions in Oki. Historical sources on the Korean side such as *Joseon Wangjo Sillok* and other sources do not confirm this fact. This *Kakusho* provides a few important clues shedding light on Ahn Yong−bok's comments and actions.

The first is one of Ahn's comments during his interrogation: "In November of *Gyeyu*(癸酉)[the Year of the Fowl], I presented the items given to me in Japan, including a volume of *Kakitsuke*(書付)[documents or memos]. They made a copy of this(癸酉十一月、日本にて下され候物共、書付の帳一冊出し申候、則寫之申候)." As *Genroku* 6 was the 'Year of the Fowl', this must have taken place when he was taken from Takeshima to Yonago.

As mentioned above, during his interrogation at *Bibyeonsa* after returning to Korea, Ahn stated that the document and silver coin received from Tottorihan had been taken away in Tsushima. However, when Ahn visited Oki once again, he testified that he brought the items or documents received in Japan back there. Furthermore, he said that *Jaihan Yakunin* made copies of those documents, but unfortunately these were not preserved.

The second point refers to events that had taken place just before Ahn came to Ulleungdo in *Genroku* 9. [The *Kakusho*] reads that just before he went to Japan, Ahn shouted at the Japanese on Ulleungdo, and chased them away saying, "Matsushima is Jasando and it is also our land(松島卽子山島, 此赤我國地)." However, as discussed above, this is not a historical fact.

Nevertheless, it is evident that he came to Japan prepared with *Paldo Chongdo* showing Takeshima and Matsushima as Korean territory.

We do not know whether he actually lodged a protest with the Lord of Oki or not. However, apart from that, since Ahn Yong−bok did come to Oki to file suit against Hakushyu (伯州へ訴訟のわけ書き出し候様に), Jaihan Yakunin demanded that Ahn put down all the details of the case, saying "書出すには及ばず、伯州へ参り委細申し上ぐべき由."

Ahn replied, "I can't write [them] down. I will tell you the details when we get to Hakushyu(書出すには及ばず、伯州へ参り委細申し上ぐべき由)." Therefore, the Yakusho of Oki was not able to notify Tottorihan of the details of the case, and was left with no choice but to inform Tottorihan that Ahn was on the way to Hoki in order to file suit.

The third point refers to when Ahn Yong–bok arrived in Aoya(青谷), having come to Hoki on June 4 with a banner across the bow of his ship reading 朝鬱兩島監稅將臣安同知騎(written using a brush). At Senenji(専念寺) Tottorihan conducted an investigation into his intentions. At *Bibyeonsa*, Ahn testified that at the time he was wearing a *Cheollik*(青帖裏), an azure blue official uniform, a *Gwan* of black cloth and leather shoes, and that he used the palanquin provided by Tottorihan. However the uniform or leather shoes were not among the items listed during the aforementioned examination of the ship when it arrived in Oki. Also, Ahn was provided with a palanquin and horse to enter the settlement around Tottori Castle. He is mistaken in thinking that this was in Aoya (青谷).

The fourth point of interest refers to when he was received at Tottorihan as a diplomatic envoy. In Aoya(青谷) he passed by the Garo(賀露), entered the settlement, and stayed in *Chōkaishō*(町會所)[the main hall]. Of course he met the *Jyūshin*(重臣)[an elder statesman] of the *Han*. Ahn said he was sitting opposite a lord when he voiced his protest about ships from Hoki sailing to Ulleungdo. In fact, he was not facing the Lord of Tottorihan. Nevertheless, we cannot deny the possibility that the petition(訴狀) Lee In-seong(李仁成) wrote under Ahn's orders was submitted to Tottorihan, sent on to the *Hantei*(藩邸) in Edo and submitted to *Shogunate*.

Eulmijo(乙未條) of *Joseon Wangjo Sillok* written in Sukjong 23 states that in February 1697(*Genroku* 10), the Lord of Tsushima posed a number of questions to the Chief of Dongrae. One of them was, "In last autumn, a person from your country submitted a petition to our authorities. Was this an order issued by your esteemed royal court?(去秋、貴國人呈單ノ事あり、朝令ニ出ヅるかと)." The Chief of Dongnae's reply is recorded as follows: "Since it is the work of a foolish person who was blown over by a storm, the Royal Court has no knowledge of them (漂風ノ愚民ニ至リテは、設ヒ作爲スル所

アルモ、朝家ノ知ル所ニ非ズ)." Further, in March of the following year, one of the documents of Chōsen Tsūkōdaiki(朝鮮通交大紀)[Great Record of Relations with Korea] recorded, "Concerning the document, it constitutes perjury.(呈書の事に至りては誠に其妄作の罪あり)" This shows that both sides, Japan and Korea, acknowledge that it was Ahn Yong−bok who submitted the petition in Japan. So, if one says he did submit the document, then it means he must have done so during his stay in Tottorihan.

The fifth point of interest refers to Ahn Yong−bok's exceedingly friendly conduct, in stark contrast to the impression we gained of him scolding and ousting the Japanese from Ulleungdo and Jasando. We find that the people of Oki also treated him amicably and with great consideration.

When the *Jaihan Yakunin*'s interrogation ended, Ahn had tried to send five bundles of dried abalone to Jaihan Yakunin and one bundle to the chief of Ookumura village (大久村). These were refused and sent back. Why had Ahn tried to send these things? Were they merely intended as gifts or had he wanted to return an earlier courtesy?

Subsequently, the Koreans said that they had not eaten dinner as the rice they had brought had run out. The Chief of Ookumura searched the ship and found that only three $G\bar{o}$(合) of rice were left. Out of pity for them, and despite it being a year of a bad harvest, he searched the village and managed to scrape together four $Sh\bar{o}$(升) and five $G\bar{o}$(合) of rice. He also provided one $T\bar{o}$(斗), two $Sh\bar{o}$ and three $G\bar{o}$ sent from Saigō(西郷). At that time, Ahn Yong−bok said that it was only proper that help should be offered to a ship rescued from being adrift. Chief of Ookumura agreed that he would help if the ship had indeed drifted here[to Japan]. He gave them rice, but only after refusing once saying that if they had planned to come here because they had 'omething to say' they should have prepared enough to eat.

In another instance, the Koreans asked to be let ashore because they were unable to write aboard their ship due to the strong daily west wind. Their request was granted, and Ahn and four men were given the nearby house of a local man. The *Kakushō* says that they stayed there from 22nd and prepared the documents for the case.

Ahn Yong-bok in Oki(隠岐)

Episodes, such as those described above, will serve as good references when thinking about Ahn Yong-bok's actions.

* The Murakami family's document 元禄九丙午年朝鮮舟着岸一巻覺書 used in this article was translated by Mr Hino Toshiharu(樋野俊晴) of Matsue City(松江市). Here I would like to express my deep gratitude for his kind help.

[Original 『北東アジア文化研究』, No. 22, pp.1-16]

A Fresh Look
at the Dokdo Issue:

Japanese Scholars Review Historical Facts

目 次

第一章

尖閣諸島と竹島問題の正しい解決
ー侵略政策の帰結としての認識が必要ー

『社會評論』23巻　2号、1997年 2月、32 - 38頁

松本健男

弁護士、人權運動, 日本 無防備地域宣言 運動 推進

尖閣諸島と竹島問題の正しい解決

——侵略政策の帰結としての認識が必要

松本 健男 _(弁護士)

（一）

日米安全保障共同宣言（一九九六年四月）は、一九六〇年の安保条約に存在していた制約をとり除き、日米間の緊密な防衛協力体制を、地域的にも、具体的内容においても飛躍的に拡大強化するものとして、これからのわが国の政治体制に重大な変更を迫るものであると理解されている。

この中には、日本周辺地域において発生しうる事態で日本の平和と安全に重要な影響を与える場合における日米間の協力に関する研究を始めることを指摘しており、またアジア・太平洋地域の不安定性の要因として、未解決の領土問題を含

めている。またその中で、「両首脳はこの地域の安定と繁栄にとり、中国が肯定的かつ建設的な役割を果たすことが死活的であることを強調し、この関連で、両国は中国との協力をさらに深めてゆくことに関心を有することを強調した」と述べているが、この短い表現の中に、日米支配勢力がアジア・太平洋地域全域に支配体制を確立する上で中国の影響力の増大を懸念していることが示されている。

この新しい政治状況の中で、これまで鎮静化していた尖閣諸島問題が再燃し、同時に、韓国との間の竹島問題が改めて浮上するに至っている。この二つの問題のいずれにおいても、日本政府の立場は、これらの島は日本固有の領土であるとす

るものだが、果してそれが正しいといえるかについて検討し、次いで、日本国民が立脚すべき基本的観点について問題を提起することとする。

（二）

尖閣諸島が日本領土である根拠として、一九七二年三月九日に外務省が発表した見解は、日本政府の公式見解と考えられる。これによれば、明治十八年（一八八五年）以降、政府が沖縄県当局を通ずる等の方法により再三にわたり現地調査を行ない、単にこれが無人島であるのみならず、清国の支配が及んでいる痕跡がないことを慎重確認の上、明治二十八年（一八九五年）一月十四日に現地に標杭を建設する旨閣議決定を行なって正式にわが国の領土である南西諸島の一部を構成した同諸島はわが国の固有の領土である。また、明治二十八年（一八九五年）発動の下関条約第二条に基づきわが国が清国から割譲を受けた台湾及び澎湖諸島には含まれていないというのである。

しかした果して政府見解がいう日本の固有領土論が正当といえるだろうか。

井上清京大教授（当時）は、一九七二年当時、幾つかの論文によって、尖閣諸島は中国領であることを解明した。その中の、『破防法研究』一六号に掲載された「いわゆる尖閣列島は中国領である」にもとづいて、同氏の見解を要約すると、

明王朝の後期に中国の福州から琉球の那覇に航海した明の皇帝の冊封使の航海記録に、釣魚諸島（尖閣諸島と同じ）の記述があり、釣魚島、黄尾嶼、赤尾嶼を経過して後に久米島（琉球所属の島）に至るとしていること、琉球王国の執政官が一六五〇年に著した琉球王国の最初の通史『琉球国中山世鑑』に右の記述を原文どおり引用していること、清朝になって以降の冊封副使がまとめた中山伝信録にも久米島が中国と琉球との境界の守りの島であることを記していること、日本人の文献でも、明治維新前に釣魚諸島について書いている林子平（江戸後期の経世家、経世済民の思想を説いた知識人。一七三八～九三年）の『三国通覧図説』の付図には、釣魚諸島を中国本土と同じ桜色にぬっていること、などの歴史的事実にもとづいて、尖閣諸島は本来、琉球とは区別された中国領土であることが論証されている、とする。

また、政府のいう日本領土編入の経緯について井上氏は次の点を指摘する。すなわち、一八八五年（明治十八年）、古賀辰四郎なる商人が新事業のための釣魚島の土地貸与を沖縄県庁に願い出たことが契機となり、内務卿山県有朋は沖縄県令に、沖縄県と清国福州との間に散在する無人島の調査を内命したが、沖縄県令は同年九月、山県内務卿に上申書を送付し、その中で、右諸島は、中山伝信録に記載した釣魚台等と同一のものである疑いがあり、踏査して直ちに国標をとりつけることには懸念があり、改めて指示賜りたい旨を記載して

いる。また山縣は同じ趣旨を外務卿井上馨にも伝達したが、井上は、近年清国側において日本政府が清国所属の島嶼を占拠した等の風説が流布し、わが国に対し猜疑を抱いているものがあるので、いま公然国標を建設する等の処置があれば、清国の疑惑を招くため、現時点では実地を踏査するにとどめるべきである旨の回答をなしている。また同年十二月には、沖縄県令に対し、国標は現時建設を要しないと心得べきとの指令がなされている。その後、一八九〇年（明治二十三年）、一八九三年（明治二十六年）、沖縄県知事は釣魚島などを同県の所轄とし、標杭を設置したい旨の上申をしたが、これに対し内務・外務大臣はこれを認める旨の指令を発していない。

結局、政府が釣魚諸島を日本領とすることに踏み切ったのは、一八九四年（明治二十七年）七月、日本海軍が宣戦布告に先立つ不意打ちで日清戦争の火ぶたが切られ、日本の勝利が確実となった同年十二月であり、翌一八九五年（明治二八年）一月十四日の閣議において、これを沖縄県所轄とし標杭を建てることを決定したのである。

以上の歴史的事実につき、井上教授は原資料をそのまま掲載して詳細な論評を加えており、右事実を否定する根拠などどこにもない。したがって先に引用した外務省見解には、これら諸島が清国の支配が及んでいない島嶼であるとする点において根本的な誤謬がある。

外務省見解は、尖閣諸島は、日清戦争の結末である下関条約によって、日本が中国から割譲を受けたものではなく、本来的な方法で取得したものだから、これを中国に返還すべきものではなく、わが国の固有の領土だとしている。しかしこのような論拠が認められるだろうか。

（三）

尖閣諸島は琉球諸島の南部にある石垣島から北方約一八〇キロ付近に東西約一〇〇キロにわたって散在している島嶼であるが、中国本土からはり出している大陸棚の東端に所在し、琉球諸島との間には水深二〇〇〇メートルの海溝が走り、その上を黒潮が両列島を分断する形で北上して流れており、その周辺は主として台湾の漁民の操業区域となっている。私たち日本在住者から見れば、沖縄諸島の一部という考えに考えられやすいが、琉球諸島との間隔は、東京～静岡、大阪～岡山よりももっと大きく、地形的にみても琉球諸島の一部ではない。前述したように、中国福建省から沖縄への航路の経路に位置しており、最東端の赤尾嶼と沖縄島西側に所在する久米島との間隔は約二二〇キロにもなっている。したがって古来、日本の住民が尖閣諸島の存在につき知悉し関心を有していたという論拠は何もない。しかし前述したとおり、わが国の支配領域の拡大を国策として追求しはじめた明治政府が古賀辰四郎の上申を契機として、その領有を企図するに至ったものであ

るが、一八九五年に至るまでの日本政府の対応は極めて慎重であった。その理由は、尖閣諸島が基本的に清国の領域内の島嶼であることが判明していることから、これを日本が領有する態度をしめすことによる紛争を恐れたことにあった。しかも右の危惧には明らかな歴史的根拠がある。すなわち、日本は日清戦争によって清国から完全な軍事的勝利をおさめるのであるが、それまでの間においては、衰退していたとはいえ、清国に対して軍事的対決によって完全な勝利をおさめうるとする確信はなかった。このことが尖閣諸島の領有の着手を躊躇した基本的な理由であった。したがって、日清戦争における決定的な軍事的勝利の後に、台湾の割譲と同時にその付属島嶼である尖閣諸島の領有を決定し完結させたのである。

この経緯を客観的に見るならば、尖閣諸島の領有は日本が軍事的侵略戦争によって獲得した台湾、澎湖諸島の領有とその本質において同一である。

第二次大戦の降伏文書によりわが国が受諾したポツダム宣言は、カイロ宣言の条項は履行せらるべくと規定し、カイロ宣言は「満州、台湾及び澎湖島のような日本国が清国より盗取したすべての地域を中華民国に返還することにある。」と規定している。前記外務省見解は、尖閣諸島は、下関条約二条に基づきわが国が清国から割譲を受けた台湾、澎湖諸島のような日本国が清国より盗取したすべての地域に含まれていない・島には含まれていないというが、満州、台湾、澎湖諸島のような日本国が清国より盗取したすべての地域に含まれていな

（四）

次に竹島についてはどう見るべきか。竹島＝独島（韓国名）は鬱陵島の東南東四九海里の日本海上に浮かぶ岩礁群であり、総面積は一辺四〇〇メートル余りの正方形に全部おさまるほどのものであるが、西島の最頂部は一七四メートルに達するけわしい岩山である。尖閣諸島とおなじく人間が常住できる条件のない無人島である。ところが日本政府は一九〇五年一月二十八日、これを竹島と名付け、本邦所属とすることを閣議決定し、その指示にしたがって島根県知事が同年二月二十二日付島根県告示四〇号をもって、「自今本県所属隠岐島司の所管」と公示する形で日本領土に編入する措置をとった。しかしこの時期がどのような時期であったかといえば、前年の一九〇四年二月にロシアへの宣戦布告がなされ、同じ二月二十三日に韓国政府に日韓議定書に調印せしめてこれを

いとどのように主張しうるのか。日本が清国に台湾、澎湖諸島を割譲させた時期と尖閣諸島を日本領土に編入することを決定実施した時期はほとんど同じであり（一八九五年四月と同年一月）、いずれも日清戦争の戦後処理として強行されたものである。こうしてみれば、日本はポツダム宣言の受諾によって、尖閣諸島を中国に返還する義務を負ったものという法的に見て到底許容されえない。べきであり、中国に対してその領有権を主張することは、国際

実質上の支配下に置くとともに、朝鮮全土を軍事占領下に置くことを実行した時期であった。日露戦争の勝利とともに、一九〇五年八月、講和条約が締結されるが、その中で日本はロシアに対し、日本が韓国において政治上軍事上および経済上卓越せる利益を有することを承認せしめており、一九〇五年十一月には、問答無用の高圧的態度をもって、韓国皇帝に対し、韓国の実質的植民地化に他ならない日韓協約書の調印を強要し、以後、日本支配の高圧的態度をもって、韓国の領土化に抗して立ち上がった義兵を徹底的に弾圧して一九一〇年の日韓併合に至るのである。したがって日本政府は韓国政府にも民衆にもまったく存在しなかったといわねばならない。

それでは竹島（独島）は本来日韓いずれの領域にあると考えられてきたのか。それについては日韓の双方に相対立する見解があるようである。その詳細に踏み込むことはできないが、大まかに考えて、韓国の所領であることに争いのない鬱陵島の付属島嶼とみなされてきたことに、韓国においては、韓国の所領である鬱陵島の付属島嶼とみなされてきており、周辺海域は主として日本の漁民の出漁場所となっていたものであり、また出雲から日本の漁民が鬱陵島に出漁した場合にその航行の目標として同島を望見していた事実が存在する。

このように、鬱陵島は面積も広く、天然資源にも恵まれ、かつ一四三〇年から約三〇〇年余、韓国政府の空島政策によって韓国人の渡航が禁止されるという時期に、日本の出雲漁民

が同島への渡航をなしていた事実が存在するが、一八八一年以降、韓国政府が鬱陵島空島化政策を改め、朝鮮本土から住民を移住させるようになり、一九〇〇年十月二十七日には韓国政府勅令四一号により郡庁に鬱陵島全島と独島を管轄させることを決定している（以上 梶村秀樹「竹島＝独島問題と日本国家」『朝鮮研究』一九七八年九月号を参照した。）こうした歴史的事実を踏まえるならば、日本政府による島根県告示の形式による日本領土への編入措置が韓国との関係において何の正当性をももたないものであることは明らかである。

それでは竹島問題は、第二次大戦の日本の降伏後の条件下においてどのように推移してきたか。一九四六年一月二十九日付の「若干の外辺地域を政治上行政上日本から分離することに関する連合国最高司令官の覚書」は、日本国外の総ての地域に関し、政治上又は行政上の権力を行使することを総て停止するよう日本帝国政府に指令したのであるが、日本の地域から除かれる地域の中に、鬱陵島、竹島、済州島を指定している。この事実は連合国が、鬱陵島、竹島、済州島と同じく、韓国に帰属している地域であると認識していたことを示している。一九五一年九月に調印されたサンフランシスコの講和条約二条の項には、「日本国は、朝鮮の独立を承認して、済州島、巨文島及び鬱陵島を含む朝鮮に対するすべての権利、権原、及び請求権を放棄する。」と規定している。講和条約の右条項につき、日本が放棄した地域から竹島を除い

は、両島とも、基本的性格において、中国もしくは韓国に所属すべきものであり、日本による領有は、国際法的に違法であることが確定している侵略の一環として理解すべきものである。したがって日本政府が一貫して強調している固有の領土論は実態的根拠を欠くものである。

しかるにわが国の政治勢力、党派は、自民・新進党はもとよりであるが、共産党においても、政府見解に追随し、中国

ているとして、竹島に対する日本の領土権は存続しているとする見解が日本では有力である。しかし、済州島、巨文島、鬱陵島は例示されているとみるべきで、竹島が付属島嶼として鬱陵島に含められているとみることは充分に可能であり、講和条約の文言を竹島の日本領土性の根拠として用いることは失当である。

韓国は日本の敗戦によってその帝国主義支配から解放され、韓国漁民は竹島に対する実効的経営の条件を回復し、出漁することになり、韓国政府は一九四九年八月の成立後、同島に行政を及ぼす公式の措置をとった。竹島の領有権問題が日韓間の重大な紛争問題として浮上したのは、一九五二年、韓国政府が海洋主権宣言を発し、竹島＝独島の周辺を含む「李ライン」を設定し、これに対し日本政府が竹島に焦点をあてて猛烈なキャンペーンを開始したことによる。一九五四年五月には、巡視船の保護の下に隠岐の漁民が集団上陸して採取活動を行なったこともあったが、韓国国会は「独島を日本人の侵攻から保全する決議」を行ない、韓国政府は五四年八月に灯台を建設するとともに警備隊を常駐させ、九六年には防波堤、埠頭工事に着手している現状にある。

　（五）

以上、尖閣諸島と竹島の歴史的事実と日本による領有化政策の基本的本質について指摘したが、結論としていえること

幻野　第39号
800円
（送料200円）

〈創作・記録〉
弔辞　　　　　　　　　　　　　　高田英太郎
修学旅行考——歴史を知る旅に篠田治美
続　甲山裁判傍聴記（二）　　　　藤沢和彦
〈詩〉
伊吹山幻想　　　　　　　　　　　吉田欣一
柘榴　　　　　　　　　　　　　　宮本善一
〈評論・随想〉
ちょっと強引な共通性
ヘミングウェイと慎太郎との
——カミュ②　　　　　　　　　　美濃山人
原泉さんと鈴子
——中野鈴子ノート　23—　　　大牧冨士夫
〈幻野雑記〉
一冊の本についてあれこれ　　　　吉田欣一
二つの「大菩薩峠」論　　　　　　永平和雄
〈雑録〉
「新島の飛騨んじい」と　　　　　永平和雄
長良川国際会議場
您好中国①⑤　　　　　　　　　　大牧冨士夫

幻野の会
岐阜県本巣郡北方町芝原中町6－23　大牧方

ならびに韓国・朝鮮民主主義人民共和国の当然の権利主張に対し、異常な敵意をもって攻撃するという許しがたい対応を示している。一九九六年九月二十二日付の『赤旗』は、尖閣諸島問題を特集しているが、「日本政府による一八九五年の編入措置は、国際的に尖閣諸島にたいする最初の領有行為であり、国際法上〈先占〉に基づく取得および実効支配とされているものです」と述べ、日本共産党は一九七二年当時から一貫して尖閣諸島が日本の領土であることを明らかにしてきたと強調している。ところが国際法上、先占とは、国家が無主の土地を占有することとされているが、この法原理自体、帝国主義列強が全世界を分割支配するための論理として登場したものであり、その法解釈において、無主の土地とは、かりに未開の土人（原文のまま）が住んでいたとしても、これらの土人（原文のまま）は国際法上の国家をも構成していないから無主の土地にほかならない（横田喜三郎 国際法Ⅱ 法律学全集 有斐閣一九七二年刊行）とするように、当該土地に居住する住民をまったく無視した強盗に等しい論理を法理化したものである。尖閣諸島にしても竹島にしても、人が居住することのできない絶海の孤島ではあるが、その周辺は付近漁民が出漁する海域であり、これら漁民にとっての生活の場として存在してきたのであり、いかなる意味においても日本が合法的にその領土としての実効的支配を行ないうるものではなかった。これを日本の領土

としたのは、中国ならびに朝鮮に対する軍事的強圧を背景に、一方的な奪取措置をとった結果であり、それを合法化するために、中国並びに朝鮮が無権限かつ無関心であったとする虚構の事実を捏造し、かつこれを前提としているにすぎない。したがって、日本政府のいう固有の領土論、ないし一部の国際法学者や日本共産党が唱える先占による合法取得という理念は、日本が一九世紀後期以来、中国ならびに朝鮮人民に加えてきた残虐極まりない暴力支配の事実を隠蔽するものであり、日本政府ならびに日本人民が国際社会において果たすべき公正な役割を自ら否定するものといわねばならない。

尖閣諸島ならびに竹島問題において、日本政府がなすべきことは、日本の領土権を撤回し、中国ならびに韓国の領土権を承認した上で、双方の利益に合致する方法での共同開発の協議や漁業海域の調整を行なうことであり、善隣友好の原則を踏まえたこうした実際的作業によって、わが国ならびに人民が受け取ることができる政治的利益は極めて大きいものといえよう。

尖閣諸島ならびに竹島問題の解決のための基本は、戦後五〇年にしてなお不変のものとして存続させようとしている政府権力のインタレストが、日本国民の中に生き続けている排他的なナショナリズムに支えられているという実体を十分に見すえ、これを克服することによって、かつてのアジア侵略が残している恥ずべき遺留物を清算することである。

第二章

竹島は日本固有領土か

『世界』2005年 6月号、53 – 63頁

內藤正中

島根大學 名譽教授,
前鳥取女子大学短期大学北東アジア總合文化研究所長兼客員教授

竹島は日本固有領土か

内藤正中

■内藤■「竹島の日」制定の波紋

韓流ブームのなか、今年は、「日韓友情年」ということで、日韓両国の友好親善は大きく進展するものと期待されていたのに、島根県議会が議員提案で上程した「竹島の日」を制定する条例が、韓国側から強い反発を受け、各地の交流事業は中止されるなど、その波紋を広げている。

竹島は島根県隠岐の島町に属している。しかし同じ島が韓国では独島と呼ばれ、慶尚北道鬱陵邑に所属する。かねてより島の領有権が争われてきた。

地元島根県としても、「島根県領土竹島の再確認」の陳情を一九五二(昭和二六)年に行って以来、ことある度にくり返してきている。したがって、何もしようとしない日本政府のヤル気を喚起するため、県独自で条例制定にふみきったものである。

島根県の地図に竹島が見られるようになったのは最近のことで、一般に県民の関心は極めて低い。独島を所管する隣国・慶尚北道が、竹島をもつ島根県とは、お互いに火種をかかえていることは承知のうえで、姉妹結縁して…五年になる。当然に地元として、竹島の研究が進められていてよいが、何故か手つかずのままできている。領土問題は国でといって棚上げして、過去の歴史に正面から向き合うことをしないできたツケがまわってきたように思われる。

それが領土問題の最前線に立つことになったのである。島根県はこれほどまでに韓国を刺激することになるとは想定もしていなかった。そこには歴史認識のズレを見ることができるわけであるが、やる以上は、それなりの勉強をしたうえでやってもらいたいと思っている。例えば、島根県が民放テレビで放映したCMも、県議会の条例案についての提案理由にしても、外務省が誤った認識をもっていることに気付かな

竹島(韓国名・独島)。
2005年3月1日撮影(AP/WWP)

外務省のホームページは、「竹島領有に関する歴史的な事実」ということで、次のように述べている。

「江戸時代の初期(一六一八年)、伯耆藩の大谷・村川両家が、幕府から鬱陵島を拝領して渡海免許を受け、毎年、同島に赴いて漁業を行い、アワビを幕府に献上していたが、竹島は

■■■ 江戸時代の竹島渡漁事業

いで、そのままを述べるだけで終わっているのである。

私は、「歴史的にも国際法上からも明らかに日本固有の領土である」という外務省の見解に疑問をもつものであり、果たしてそうであるかを検証してゆくことにしたい。

鬱陵島渡航への寄港地、漁労地として利用されていた。また、遅くとも一六六一年には、両家は幕府から竹島を拝領してい

この記述をもとに、外務省は「我が国は、遅くとも一七世紀半ばには、実効的支配に基づき竹島の領有権を確立していたと考えられる」というが、そのように断定できるかどうか。

まず第一に、「伯耆藩」などという藩は存在しなかったことである。因幡・伯耆両国を領有し、鳥取に居城を定めていたことから、鳥取藩とか因州藩と呼ぶのが通例である。韓国側が「伯耆州」といっているのに影響されたとすれば情けない。

第二には、鬱陵島と竹島を幕府から「拝領」したというが、これは明らかに間違っている。ここで外務省がいっている竹島は当時松島と呼ばれていた現在の竹島のことであるが、当時は一般に鬱陵島を竹島と呼んでいたので、本稿ではその竹島(鬱陵島)・松島(現竹島)を使う。幕府から拝領したというのは、大谷家文書に見えるが、一一代の当主が一八二〇年代(文政年間)にまとめた「竹島渡海由来記抜書控」からとっている。大谷家は火事で文書のほとんどを焼失し、残った文書を集めてこの「抜書控」を作成した。「拝領」の文言は、一六八一(延宝九)年に三代当主が巡見使に回答した御請書のなかに出てくるが、すべての土地は領主のものという封建社会・では、幕府が町人に島を分与するなどはありえないというべ

きである。

第三に、幕府が許可したのは竹島(鬱陵島)への渡海だけで、松島(現竹島)渡海については、「幕府の内意」を得たにすぎないと、川上健三も記している(『竹島の歴史地理学的研究』一九六六年)。川上は外務省条約局にあって、調査官として、竹島が日本固有領土であるという説を歴史的に解明する作業に従事した。

外務省がいうように、鬱陵島を町人に拝領させたのであれば、それは日本領となり、渡海をするのに特別許可は必要ない。わざわざ申請し、幕府が鳥取藩主宛に許可したのは、あるいは朝鮮領ではないかという危惧があったからである。直前の一六一四(慶長一九)年に、対馬藩が鬱陵島を磯竹島と称して領有化を画策し、朝鮮政府から強く抗議される事件があった。この時、朝鮮国との往来は対馬経由の航路だけで、他の道をとって来航する者は海賊とみなすという申し入れを受けていた。したがって竹島に渡海しようという米子町人に対して、幕府としては外国貿易を許可する朱印状は出すことができず、奉書のかたちで認めたと思われる。

御奉書というのは、海外渡航をする本人で、竹島渡海のように藩主に宛てたものは例外である。しかも幕府が許可したのは「今度渡海」と記してあるように、今度の渡海だけである。そうである以上は、渡海ごとに申請しなければならなかったはずであるが、大谷家に残っているのは初回だけで、それも写しである。このことからいえるのは、幕府が竹島を日本領とみなして竹島行きを国内並みに取扱ったのではないかということである。

さらに問題となるのは、許可した年を一六一八(元和四)年と決めてかかってよいかということである。大谷家の「抜書控」で「元和四年より渡海はじまる」と記してあることから、一六一八年が通説になり、外務省もそう記す。しかし幕府の奉書には、「五月一六日」とあるだけで年号はない。しかも署名している四名のうち、老中職にあるのは二名だけで、他の二名は小姓組番頭であった。四名がそろって老中になるのは一六二二(元和八)年であり、当然に奉書を発給したのはその年以降としなければならないはずである。

松島と呼ばれた現竹島の「拝領」について、外務省が一六六一(寛文元)年と断定しているのもおかしい。一六六一年は川上健三が推定したもので、「寛文元年の松島渡海」というのは、大谷、村川両家が幕府の正式承認の下に、同島におもむくようになった年を意味しているようにも考えられる」と述べていることによる。大谷家文書では渡海した年をいくつかあげているが、それは松島に行くようになったというものに

ないとう・せいちゅう　一九二九年岡山県生まれ。島根大学名誉教授。著書に、『島根県の百年』『日本海地域の在日朝鮮人』『鳥取県の歴史』、『竹島(鬱陵島)をめぐる日朝関係史』など。

すぎず、川上も「幕府の内意を得て」と記すにとどめている
のである。それをもって・一六六一年には、両家は幕府から
拝領していた」などといえるわけもない。

■■■■
竹島渡海禁止と松島

米子町人による竹島(鬱陵島)渡海事業は、元和年間から七
〇年以上にわたってつづけられ、アワビやアシカ油、銘木、
薬草などを持ち帰り珍重されていた。しかし幕府に対しては
「貢物上納仕らず」であり、代りに幕府役人に申アワビを献
上したり、注文にこたえて銘木などを贈っていた。また鳥取
藩としては、渡海費用として毎年米千俵を貸与、御城銀を貸
付けるなどして支援をし、申アワビを藩が買上げて清算してい
た。

このため竹島は、伯耆国に属する島と思われるようになり、
一六六七(寛文七)年に松江藩の斉藤豊仙がまとめた『隠州視
聴合紀』には、隠岐国の西北に竹島と松島があることが記さ
れる。この史料は、松島(現竹島)のことが初めて記された
ものとして注目されているが、竹島(鬱陵島)を日本の西北端と
みるか、隠岐を当てるかで、日韓両国間では意見が対立して
いる。私は、竹島渡海の最盛期であり、隠岐の人たちも伯耆
国に属する日本領として竹島(鬱陵島)をみていたと思って
いる。またそうでなければ、三〇〇年後に日朝両国間で争う「竹
島〇一件」と呼ばれる領土紛争の意味がない。

「竹島一件」の結末は、竹島すなわち鬱陵島が朝鮮の領土
であることを確認したことである。朝鮮政府は一五世紀以来、
島に人がいたら倭寇が攻めてくるといって、鬱陵島を無人に
する空島政策をとってきていたが、もちろん領有権を放棄し
たわけではない。米子町人は無人島であるために渡海事業を
つづけることができたが、それは空島に持主の了解なしに入
り込み、宝物を奪って帰るに似た行為といわねばならず、そ
うした泥棒行為を外務省のホームページのように、「我が国
は、遅くとも一七世紀半ばには、実効的支配に基づく竹島の
領有権を確立していた」というわけにはゆかないのである。

米子町人の竹島渡海に行ってみると、すでに朝
鮮人が来ていた。その年に竹島に朝鮮側が抗議したのが一六九三(元
禄六)年であった。そこで証拠になる笠や頭巾をもって帰り藩
庁に報告、鳥取藩では幕府に対処を求めた。

翌年も朝鮮人が先に来ていた。そのなかの二人を捕えて米
子に連行、二か月も拘留したのち、幕府の指示で長崎に送り、
対馬藩から帰国させた。この時幕府は対馬藩に命じて、竹島
への朝鮮人の通漁を禁止するようにと、朝鮮政府に申し入れ
をした。

これに対して朝鮮側は、「倭人のいう竹島は我が国の鬱陵
島である」と主張し、「竹島一件」といわれている外交接渉
が三年間にわたって行われた。結局、一六九六(元禄九)年一
月二八日に、幕府が竹島渡海を禁止し、その旨を鳥取藩に達

した。

このことに関連して外務省のホームページは、現竹島（松島）への渡航禁止は言及しなかったとする。しかし松島については、竹島に附属する島として特段の取扱いはしておらず、渡海免許を与えていない松島の往復途中に言及する必要はなかったのである。松島は、竹島の往復途中に望見したり立ち寄るくらいで、竹島渡海が禁止されれば、松島へだけ行く者はなかった。

とりわけて重要なのは、幕府の竹島渡海禁止を決定づけたと思われる、一六九五（元禄八）年一二月二五日付で幕府に提出した鳥取藩の回答書である。

一二月二四日に老中阿部豊後守から、鳥取藩に竹島関連で七か条の質問が発せられている。その第一は、「因州伯州に付属する竹島はいつから附属になったか」というもので、鳥取藩はこれに「竹島は因幡伯耆に附属するものではない」と回答した。そして第七項で、「竹島の外に両国附属の島があるか」との質問に対しては、「竹島松島其外両国附属の島はない」と答えているのである。鳥取藩が、竹島とともに松島（現竹島）についても、因伯両国附属のものではないとしたことは重要で、すなわち日本領とはいえない松島についても、竹島波海禁止令の例外とするわけにはゆかないことは明らかである。

竹島と呼んできた鬱陵島が朝鮮領とされた以上、その属島とみられている松島（現竹島）も朝鮮領となる。

日本側は、竹島に行く途中に松島があることを知っていた。しかし韓国側は、鬱陵島の于山国が五一二年に新羅に服属した記録はあるが、独島関係のものはない。鬱陵島とは別の島が東海にあることが知られるのは、一五世紀半ばの于山島からで、『世宗実録地理志』（一四三二年）の蔚珍県の条に「于山、武陵二島は県の正東の海中に在り、二島去ること遠からず、風が吹き清明な時には望見できる」とある。しかし鬱陵島には空島政策がとられていたので、時たま派遣された官員の報告が記録されているだけで、民間情報もなく、于山島を実地にたしかめることもなかった。

したがって、一五三一年刊の『新増東国與地勝覧』の江原道図のように、鬱陵島と同じ大きさで、その西方に于山島を記したりする。この于山島をはじめ、三峯島、可支島などがあるといわれているが、それらを現在の独島に比定することはできない。しかし一六九六（元禄九）年に、鳥取藩に抗議するために来日した東莱の安龍福が、鬱陵島とは別の島を于山島といった背景には、それなりの情報が広く流布されていたとみなければなるまい。

安龍福の来日は、独島の領有権が朝鮮国にあることを幕府

に確認させたということで、韓国では中学高校の国史教科書で特筆大書されている。ところが日本では、官名詐称の狂言とか、虚言癖のある私人の単独行動であるとか、安龍福の抗議来藩を過小に評価し、鳥取藩にとっては重要な外交問題であったにもかかわらず、「鳥取県史」でさえも言及していない。

この問題についての韓国側史料は、『朝鮮王朝実録』、その他であり、帰国後捕えられて備辺司で訊問された供述が記してある。すなわち安龍福が鬱陵島で日本人を見つけ、干山島まで追いかけた時、「松島は即ち子山島、これ亦我が国地」といったことになっている。子山島は于山島である。しかしその年には、一月に竹島渡海禁止令が出されていたため、米子町人は出かけていないのであるから、安龍福の発言と行動は作りごととなる。

鳥取藩の側には、安龍福が伯耆国に到着してから二か月の間の状況を詳細に記した史料がある。私もかつて『竹島(鬱陵島)をめぐる日朝関係史』(二〇〇〇年、多賀出版)のなかで記しておいた。両国にまたがる事件である以上、両国の史料をつき合わせて解明すべきであって、韓国側のように、自国の史料だけに頼る手法は、一国主義的歴史観であるといって批判した。

伯耆国にやって来た安龍福は、「朝鬱両島監税将臣安同知騎」と墨書した旗をかかげていた。ここでの「朝鬱両島」と

は「鬱陵島ト于山島是ナリ」と、一八二八(文政一二)年に鳥取藩士岡嶋正義の「竹島考」は注記している。

また安龍福が、伯耆州(鳥取藩主)から「両島既属国」と、鬱陵、干山両島が朝鮮領であるとする書契を取りつけたことも、『朝鮮王朝実録』にはみられるが、鳥取城下に迎えられて外交使節として処遇はされたが、鳥取藩主に会った事実はないから、書契などもらえるはずもない。ただ鳥取藩を通じて将軍に宛てた訴状を提出し、そこで言及していた可能性についてまで否定することはできないであろう。それというのも、釜山での交渉で対馬藩主は東莱府使に、「去る秋、貴国人呈単の事あり」と告げているし、朝鮮側でも「漂風ノ愚民」による「呈書ノ事」があったことを認めているのである。

このようにみてくると、鳥取藩に抗議するために来日した安龍福によって、鬱陵島の東方に干山島があり、両島ともに朝鮮の領土であると主張した事実は認めなければならないと思われる。

■■■明治新政府の決定

明治維新後、新政府は朝鮮国に外務省官員を派遣して、一八七〇(明治三)年に『朝鮮国交際始末内探書』と題する報告書を受けた。そこでは、「竹島松島朝鮮附属ニ相成候始末」として、「松島ハ竹島ノ隣島ニテ、松島ノ儀ニ付是迄掲載セシ書留モコレナク」、竹島については「元禄度後ハ暫クノ間セ

シテ、其ノ地方ノ小島竹島ト稱スル者アレ共、一個ノ岩石ニ過キサル旨ヲ知リ、多年ノ疑義一朝氷解セリ」と結論づけたことを、北島正誠の『竹島考證』（一九六六年、復刻版）は記している。

■■■ 大韓帝国勅令第四一号

一九〇〇（明治三三）年一〇月二五日付大韓帝国勅令第四一号は、鬱陵島を鬱島と改称し、島監を郡守に改めて郡制を施行する。そして鬱島郡は鬱陵島のほか、竹島、石島を管轄するとした。ここでの竹島は鬱陵島近くの竹嶼島のことで、石島が独島に当たると韓国側はいっている。その当時、島民の多くが全羅道出身者で、全羅道方言では石を独と発音しているのでトル島としたわけで、発音通りならば独島になるという。

関連して、一九〇四（明治三七）年九月二五日の軍艦新高の航海日誌が、松島（現竹島）に行ってリアンコルド岩実見者より聞いた話として、「リアンコルド岩、韓人之ヲ独島ト書シ、本邦漁夫之ヲ略シテリアンコ島ト呼稱セリ」と記しているように、韓国人が漢字で書く場合は、石島ではなく独島と記すとする。

このように、石島が独島であり、鬱島郡に属する島であることを認識していたからこそ、一九〇六（明治三九）年に島根県の神西部長ら一行が立ち寄って、リアンコ島の領土編入のことを郡守の沈興澤に告げた時、郡守は本郡所属の独島が日

本領にされたことに驚いて、直ちに江原道庁に報告して対処を求めたのである。」

一九〇〇〈明治三三〉年のこの勅令が、石島すなわち独島を韓国領としていたことが確認できれば、一九〇五〈明治三八〉年のリアンコ島の日本領土編入は「無主地先占」というわけにはゆかなくなる。

この当時、日本政府関係者がリアンコ島が韓国領であることを知らなかったとは思われないのである。いくつかの例証をあげておく。まず地理学者田渕友彦の『韓国新地理』(一九〇五年)は、江原道鬱陵島の項目で「ヤンコ島」として記している。

領土編入を申請した中井養三郎も、「此の島を朝鮮の領土と信じて」韓国政府に貸下申請を行うつもりで上京した〈奥原碧雲『竹島及鬱陵島』一九〇七年〉。中井からの申請を受けた内務省地方局では、「韓国領地ノ疑アル莫荒タル一個不毛ノ岩礁ヲ収メテ、環視ノ諸外国ニ我ガ国ガ韓国併呑ノ野心アルコトノ疑ヲ大ナラシムル」といって却下している〈島根県広報文書課『竹島関係資料』第一巻〉。

■■■ リアンコ島の日本領土編入

一九〇四〈明治三七〉年秋、上京した島根県西郷町の中井養三郎は、内務省で申請を拒否されたのち、外務省で山座円次郎政務局長に面会する。山座は「時局ナレバコソ其領土編入ヲ急務トスルナリ」と述べて、外交上では問題はなく、内務

省のような心配は無用とした。山座はソウルの日本公使館にいた韓国通である。さらに農商務省水産局長牧朴真、海軍省水路局長肝付兼行らと協議して、内務、外務、農商務三大臣に宛て「りゃんこ島領土編入並ニ貸下願」を提出させた。なかでも海軍省の肝付局長は、「肝付将軍断定ニ頼リテ本島ノ全ク無所属ナルコトヲ確カメタリ」ということで、中井が前年からリアンコ島でアシカ漁をはじめたことをもって、「同島経営ニ従事セルモノナル以上ハ」といって、「無主地先占」の理論を適用して領土編入することを提案した。

すでに日露戦争は始まっている。六月には対馬海峡で陸軍輸送船が撃沈されるなど、ウラジオストク艦隊の南下が危惧され、海軍は韓国東海岸に監視所を設けて海底電信線で結ぶこととし、鬱陵島との問も九月には開通した。だから外務省の山座局長は、リアンコ島〈竹島〉に望楼を設けて海底電線を敷設すれば、「敵艦艦上極メテ屈意ナラズヤ」といって、領土編入が急務であると説く。

一九〇五年一月八日の閣議決定は、以下の内容をもっていた。

「別紙内務大臣請議無人島所属ニ関スル件ヲ審査スルニ……無人島ハ他国ニ於テ之ヲ占領シタルト認ムヘキ形跡ナク……明治三十六年以来中井養三郎ナル者該島ニ移住シ漁業ニ従事セルコトハ関係書類ニ依リ明ナル所ナレバ、国際法上占領ノ事実アルモノト認メ之ヲ本邦所属トナシ……」

無人の島が所属不詳というのは明らかに一方的な独断である。前述のように、五年前の一九〇〇(明治三三)年には大韓帝国勅令が公布されている。内務省が「韓国領地ノ疑アル」といっていたこととも関連する。また中井がリアンコ島に対して松島と呼んでいたことを捨て去り、フランスの捕鯨船が命名したリアンクール岩(リアンコ島)を島名にして怪しまなかったのは何故か。

新島命名の事情もおかしい。島根県内務部長から意見を求められた隠岐島司が、歴史的背景を無視して、鬱陵島を竹島と呼んでいるのは「誤称」だとして、海図では松島となっているので(シーボルトの誤解による)、新島は竹島と命名すべしと回答したことである。島の命名理由からすれば、江戸期と同じように竹島ではなく松島とすべきであった。このことについて島根県庁内では誰からも異議が出されず、島司の回答通り竹島ということで内務省に報告され、そのまま閣議で決定されたのである。新島竹島についての認識が、地元でも如何に稀薄なものであったかを知ることができるわけで、そんなものが固有領土といえるだろうか。

ここでの領土編入を考える場合、日露戦争のさなかで、日本軍隊が韓国内に駐留していた時のことであることに留意すべきである。

一九〇四(明治三七)年二月一〇日に日本はロシアに宣戦を布告、同月二三日には「日韓議定書」を

たことはあるが、日本領だと主張したことは一度もなかった。

領有意思の再確認にはならないのである。むしろ日本側に領有意識がなかった例として、その島名をあげることができる。江戸期には、現竹島を鬱陵島の竹島に対して松島と呼んでいたことを示すものである。

「移住」して漁業に従事していたというが、小屋を仮設して漁期にだけ出漁していたにすぎず、移住といえる実態はなかった。軍艦対馬の報告も、十日間ばかりの「仮居」であったという。無主地先占というが、無主地ならば固有領土説と矛盾するし、先占の実情は右の如くであった。

だから外務省のホームページは領有権の再確認説をとる。すなわち、「閣議決定及び島根県告示による竹島の島根県への編入措置は、日本政府が近代国家として竹島を領有する意思を再確認したものであり、……また当時、新聞にも掲載され、秘密裡に行われたものではないなど、有効に実施されたものである」。

ところが、閣議で決定した領土編入を関係国に通報することとも、官報による公示もなく、編入措置をとった島根県に対して、「管内への公示」を示達しただけであったから、韓国側は先占は無効であると主張する。

さらに、歴史的に日本の固有領土であったというが、すでにみたように、一六九六(元禄九)年と一八七七(明治一〇)年の二度にわたって、日本には関係がない島であると決めている。したがって、江戸期以来リアンコ島の領有権について否認し

締結する。それは、仁川に上陸した日本軍がソウルに入り、韓国の首都を軍事的に制圧したうえでの締結であった。韓国の施政は日本の指導下に置かれ、日本軍は軍略上で必要とする地を臨機収容することができるようになり、駐留権と土地収容権を確保する。さらに五月三一日には、「対韓施設綱領」を閣議決定し、韓国の保護国化を明確に方向づけ、八月二二日の第一次日韓協約で財政と外交の顧問を韓国政府が雇い入れることを定めた。

そして一九〇五(明治三八)年一月の旅順攻略につづき、三月の奉天会戦、五月の日本海海戦をひかえた一月二八日に、リアンコ島の領土編入を日本政府は閣議で決定したのである。外務省の山座政務局長、海軍省の肝付水路局長が積極的役割を果たしたことは前述した通り。しかも一月からはソウル・一帯の治安警察権は、日本軍が掌握するという戦時体制下での領土編入であった。したがって韓国政府に通告していたとしても、それに異議を申し立てるような状況にはなかったというべきで、初めから無視していたと考えた方がよい。日露講和後の一一月一七日には第二次日韓協約であり、一二月二〇日からは韓国統監府が設置され、韓国の日本による保護国化は確実に進められてゆく。

日本の竹島領有一〇〇年は、韓国にとっては日帝支配の植民地化がはじまる一〇〇年であり、日本による独島領有はその第一歩ということになる。

■■■ 未解決の竹島問題

一九四三(昭和一八)年のカイロ宣言は、日本が暴力的に略取した新附の領土は返還させると定めていた。固有領土は除外されるため、川上健三らによる竹島研究がはじめられ、『竹島の歴史地理学的研究』がまとめられた。

日本占領の連合国軍総司令部は、一九四六(昭和二一)年の覚書六七七号で、日本政府の行政権行使が停止される地域に取った新附の領土は竹島を含めていた。また同年の覚書一〇三三号でも日本船の操業許可区域の外に竹島を位置づけていた。ただこれらの覚書は、領土帰属の最終的決定ではないときれており、一九五二(昭和二七)年に対日平和条約が発効するとともに、必然的に効力を失ったとする立場からは、竹島は平和条約で日本領土になったと理解する。

しかし覚書一〇三三号が平和条約発効の三日前に廃止が通告されていることから、すべての覚書が自動的に無効になったというのは誤りであるとする説もある。竹島について明示的に規定されているのは覚書六七七号だけであり、対日平和条約がそれと矛盾するはずはなく、実質的な変更はなかったと韓国側は主張する。

ここでの問題も、極東における冷戦激化の状況に対処しようとしたアメリカの意図が具体化されたことにある。

一九四九(昭和二四)年九月にはソ連が原爆保有を発表した。

一〇月には親米的な中華民国に代って中華人民共和国が成立する。そして一九五〇年には朝鮮戦争の勃発である。米ソ対立の冷戦が極東でも広がるなかで、アメリカは対日講和を促進するため、国務省顧問のダレスは予備交渉を開始させるのであった。「平和国家日本」に国際して再軍備に消極的であった日本を説得し、アメリカの味方に立たせることがねらいであった。川上はこれを「極東における秩序の安定を目途」にして対日平和条約草案の領域区分が進められたとみている。

一九四九年一一月二日付草案までは、竹島は朝鮮領になっていた。それをみた駐口米国政治顧問のシーボルトが、国務省に対して竹島の帰属を再考するよう提案した。彼は「安全保障の考慮がこの地に気象及びレーダー局を想定する」と述べている。こうして四九年一二月二九日付草案からは、竹島は日本領に変えられる。この時イギリス、ニュージーランドは竹島を日本の領域外に置いていたが、ダレスはそれを説得して最終案をまとめた。

当然に韓国は反発した。独島を明記するように要求したが、アメリカは、「かつて朝鮮によって領土主張がなされたとは思われない」といって受け入れなかった。日本が固有領土説を主張した「外交的成果」である。しかし韓国も負けられない。独島を日本領土からは明白に除外し、韓国領であることをアメリカが「黙示的に承認した」と、当時外務部政務局長

であった金東祚は述べている。アメリカのダブルスタンダードが問題をあいまいなままにして結着させたといってよい。

アメリカが主導して作成した対日平和条約には、竹島について書かれていない。そのため日韓両国には異なる解釈をする。だから外務省にいて固有領土説を主張してきた川上も、著書の「あとがき」で当面して竹島の問題は「未解決」と記さざるをえなかったのである。そこには戦後史の問題や国際法での論点解明が課題として残されていることを示している。

ともあれ、歴史にかかわる問題については、本稿で述べてきた通りである。竹島研究で川上の著書は古典的といってよいほどのものであるが、刊行以来四十年近くを経過した現在、当然に川上の研究を批判的に乗りこえる成果もあげられてきている。そうした研究成果を無視している外務省の不勉強は許すわけにはゆかないのである。

竹島問題は日韓両国にまたがっている課題である。そうである以上、両国の関係係史料をつき合わせて共通の土俵をくって客観的な立場で解明してゆく必要に迫られている。すでに韓国では宋炳基編「独島領有権史料選」(二〇〇四年、ハンリム大学校アジア文化研究所)のように、日本側の史料のままで収録した史料集も刊行されるようになった。歴史の問題である以上、歴史の事実を確認し、それを尊重することからはじめられなければならないと思っている。

第三章

前近代竹島の歴史學的研究序説

『靑丘學研究論集』25. 2001年 3月. 147‒184頁

池內敏

名古屋大學大學院文學研究科教授

はじめに

寛文七年（一六六七）に出雲藩士斎藤豊仙が著した「隠州視聴合紀」の冒頭「国代記」にある記述をめぐり、これまでいくつか議論が重ねられてきた。それは戦後の竹島／独島をめぐる日韓交渉と密接に関わるかたちで問題提起されたから、いきおい政治色を帯びた議論ともなった。その焦点は、端的に述べれば「然則日本之乾地、以二此州一為レ限矣」とする文中の「此州」が、欝陵嶋（江戸時代における竹島）を指すのか、隠州を指すのか、というところにあった。韓国政府側は隠州として対立したこともあって、解釈は政治的に引きずられ、厳密な解釈というよりむしろ恣意に流れる傾向も皆無ではなかった。しかも議論には感情的な応酬も混じり込み、史料解釈としてはテクスト自体から離れてゆく傾向が否定できない。

そこで本稿では、政治的な意図から離れてテクストに立ち戻り、史料に即して解釈するとどのように読まざるを得ないか、について再検討したい。その際、『続々群書類従』第九に収録されたものを底本に、『日本庶民生活史料集成』第二十巻に収録されたもの等を参照しつつ、以下検討する。

一、「隠州視聴合紀」の構成・内容・用語法

「隠州視聴合紀」の全体構成は、序および巻一「国代記」・巻二「周吉郡」・巻三「穏地郡」・巻四「嶋前紀」から成る。隠岐国は大きく嶋前・嶋後に分けられるが、巻一「国代記」が隠岐国全体を扱い、巻二・三が嶋後に属する周吉郡・穏地郡について、巻二・三が嶋後に属する周吉郡・穏地郡について、郷・村・里の単位で地理的特徴を述べ、それぞれの単位ごとに名所・旧跡や故事を記す。同様に巻四では嶋前に属する知夫郡・海部郡内の郷・村・里について記し、さらに延喜格式神名帳・国中仏寺・名所和歌・知夫郡焼火山縁起・文覚論もここに含まれる。

すなわちこれまで議論の対象とされてきた巻一「国代記」とは、郷・村・里単位に細分されて記された巻二～四に対し、国単位で見た場合の特性を記した部分といえる。そこで「国代記」の内容を確認するため、句読点を付しながら、少し長めに史料引用してみたい。その際、意味のまとまりを鮮明にするために適宜改行して示す。

[史料二][3]

隠州在二北海中一、故[4]隠岐嶋（割注）「按、倭訓海中言二遠幾一（ヲキ）、故名歟」、其在二巽地一（チブリ）[5]言二島前一也、知夫郡・海部郡（アマ）属レ焉、其位二震地一（シキ）[6]言二島後一、周吉郡・穏地郡（オチ）属レ焉、其府者（ソンフ）周吉郡南岸西郷豊崎也、従二是南一（ノ方）至二伯州赤碕浦一四十里、未申至二三十五里、辰巳（ノ方）至二伯州温泉津一五十八里、自レ子至レ卯無二可往地一、戌亥間行二日一夜有二松島一、又一日程有二竹島一（俗言二磯竹一）[7]、此二島無二人之地一、見二高麗一如下自二雲州一望中隠岐上一[8]、然則日本之乾地、以二此州一為レ限矣[9]、

民部図帳日、凡諸健児免二徭役一、隠岐国以二三国造田三町地一子レ充レ之、然近代所レ賦毎年一萬千六百余斛一、其余又以二漆・椿実（キノミ）・山椒（ノ）・紫藻（アハビ）・鯛・鰯（イカ）・鰒（トヒウ）・鯖・石決明・烏賊・馬皮等一、是慶長年中堀尾氏之所レ定也、

古老伝日、昔対馬守源義親之国也、其後薩摩守忠教在二雲州美保関一領レ之、（割注）「忠度城跡在二三保一」、其後鎌倉右大将家使下二地頭人一治上レ之、（中略）嗚呼此何年、始封以来四百八十余年、時永禄某年七月、其後自二芸州一使下猪頭九郎・岡野木工等二守護于此上一也、此時始置二館於矢尾一居レ之、後経三十八年一、毛利氏去、堀尾氏領レ之、過二二世

三十五年二而亡一、又京極若州大守領レ之、一世四年而亡、遂帰二萬々世一矣、

さて、右に引用したように、「国代記」は概ね三つの内容から構成される。「隠州在二北海中一」から「然則日本之乾之地、以二此州一為レ限矣」までが隠岐国の地理的特性を述べた部分、「民部図帳日」から「是慶長年中堀尾氏之所レ定也」までが隠岐国に賦課された貢納物（物産と言い換えうるかもしれない）について述べた部分、そして「古老伝日」から「遂帰二萬々世一矣」までが隠岐国の歴史（源義親から京極氏に到る隠岐国を支配した武将の変遷）である。

こうした三部構成をとるなかの、地理的特性を述べた冒頭部分のみがこれまで着目され、「国代記」の他の部分や「隠州視聴合紀」全体から切り離されて解釈、議論がなされてきた。斎藤豊仙の記述態度や文体が、当該冒頭部分のみ他の部分から独立していると考えるのは不自然であり、彼の意図や内容を理解するためには、「国代記」の他の部分や「隠州視聴合紀」全体の記述との整合性をも勘案しながら解釈することが不可欠と思われる。

さて、議論となっている冒頭部分は以下のように釈読されねばなるまい。ただし最後の一文にある「此州」については、

「州」の解釈をめぐる議論が分かれているため、とりあえず「州」という表記のまま残しておく。

（一―一）隠岐国は北海中にあるがゆえに（島名を）隠岐嶋という。按ずるに、倭訓に海中を遠幾（おき）というゆえの名か。

（一―二）隠岐国のうち）南東にあるものを島前というなり。知夫郡・海部郡これに属す。

（一―三）隠岐国のうち）東にくらいする（位置する）を島後という。周吉郡・穏地郡これに属す。

（一―四）その（隠岐国の）府は周吉郡南岸西郷豊崎なり。

（二―一）これ（隠岐国）より南は、出雲国美穂関に至ること三十五里、

（二―二）（隠岐国より）南東は、伯耆国赤碕浦に至ること四十里、

（二―三）（隠岐国より）南西は、石見国温泉津に至ること五十八里、

（二―四）（隠岐国より）北から東に至る往くべき地無し。

（二―五―一）（隠岐国より）戌と亥のあいだの方角（概ね北西方向）へ行くこと二日一夜にして松島あり、

（二―五―二）そこ（松島）からさらに一日ほどで竹島あ

り。俗に磯竹島という。竹・魚・海鹿、多し。〔按ずるに、神言にいういわゆる五十猛か。〕

（二―五―三）この二島（松島・竹島）は人無きの地、高麗を見ること雲州より隠岐を望むが如し。

（三）そうであるならば則ち、日本の北西の地はこの州をもって限りとす。

右に見るように、「国代記」冒頭の地理的特性を述べた部分は、隠岐国の構成について述べた部分（一―一～四）、隠岐国を基点にして四方位に何があるかを述べた部分（二―一～五）、（三）を踏まえて日本（の本土）と隠岐国との位置関係を述べた部分（三）の、三つの内容から構成されることが明瞭である。

先述したように、「国代記」は、国単位で見た隠岐国の特性を記したものであり、地理・貢納・歴史の三部構成をとる。右に整理した（三）の部分は、次の項目（貢納）に移行する直前にあって、隠岐国の国単位での地理的特性を述べるに際して締まりをつける部分にあたっている。こうした点に鑑みて史料を素直に解釈しようとすれば、（三）にある「此州」が何を指しているかは自ずから明瞭であり、議論の生じようはずもない。

にもかかわらず議論が決着しない根本原因を突き詰めてみれば、「州」は「島（嶋）」と読み替えても良い、とする主張にゆきあたる。管見の限りでは、そうした主張は「州はシマの意である」とする［田川孝三、四三頁］に遡る。その見解が再検討されることもなく踏襲されているところに議論混迷の要因があるように思われてならない。

さて、表1は『隠州視聴合紀』における「州」および「島（嶋）」の用例をすべて検索し、整理したものである。このうち、「州」の用例についてみてみると、「隠州視聴合紀」全体から六六例を見いだすことができ、うち六〇例が、隠岐国・出雲国といった特定の国名を隠州・雲州などと略称する事例であることが分かる。それ以外の六例について、その事例が登場する前後の範囲をとって、以下登場順に掲げる（傍線は引用者、以下同様）。

A 戊亥間行二日一夜有三松島一、又一日程有三竹島一、此二島無レ人之地、見三高麗一如下自二雲州一望中隠岐上、然則日本之乾之地、以二此州一為レ限矣、（『続々群書類従』第九、四五〇頁上段）

B 雲州刺史尼子伊予守者、佐々木之棟梁、隣州之盟主也、（同前、四五〇頁下段）

C 聞三元就欲レ討二隠州一…（中略）…為三清之旧臣一（個人名五人省略）潜偶語而曰、清家雖三令弟一本比肩之家人（也）、五郎君雖三幼弱一佐々木之根本也、以二才又郎（仮）元就威、以至二此州一則吾儕皆渠之馬卒也、（同前、四五一頁上段～下段、なお（　）内は『日本庶民史料集成』本による）

D 一国悉奉三五郎君一為三主君一、寺本等威権行二内外一、莫レ曽達二於心一者レ、又五郎人聞レ之、泣告二元就一曰、我生不レ可レ戴レ天、若以三君之霊一賜三命世上一、乃請労二百騎一、自則招二旧交人一対二隠州一、以レ其地一為二付庸一、長守二藩屏一、言與レ涙倶也、元就憫レ之以二百余騎一与レ之、才又郎大悦到二雲州笠浦一、䁗二於隠州動静一、雖レ然風波難レ期送二数日一、此時二州人一以三五郎君之年少一最夕遊宴軍制相忘、不レ問二津口之出入一也、（同前、四五二頁上段）

E 昔鄭交題二古塚一曰、塚上雨竿（竹）、風吹常裊々、塚中有レ声曰、下有二百年人一長睡不レ知レ暁于漢于レ和有レ似矣哉、又此州之老或有下称三村上天皇之末孫一而号中村上某上、問三其所一由出一則曰、唐橋之遺腹也、（同前、四六一頁下段、なお〔　〕内は『日本庶民生活史料集成』本による）

表1　『隠州視聴合紀』における「州」「島（嶋）」の用例

「州」の用例	
国代記	特定国名36（隠州11、雲州11、芸州6、若州3、伯州2、但州2、石州） 此州2、隣州、一州
巻2以後	特定国名24（隠州9、雲州7、伯州3、因州、但州、勢州、若州、豆州） 此州2
計	特定国名60 此州4、隣州、一州

「島（嶋）」の用例	
国代記	必ずしも島名とはいえない地名等12（島前6、島後4、島根郡2） 特定島名4（隠岐島、松島、竹島、磯竹島） その他2（此二島、孤島）
巻2以後	必ずしも島名とはいえない地名等17（島前7、島後4、新島守2、島崎、島神、島地、敷島） 特定島名72（松島3、白島3、渡島2、磯竹島2、冠島2、籬島2、白戸島2、篷島2、赤島2、小峰島2、黒島2、長島、青島、鴎島、中島、甲島、琴島、小敷島、烏帽子島、鴉島、小白島、帆掛島、屏島、田島、沖島、左婦島、姫島、雀島、鶴島、貝島、平島、神島、前平島、大形島、賎木島、大守島、宇津島、柱島、神の島、恩部島、平瀬島、大領島、巫島、見付島、立島、膝島、雁島、麻島、駄島、伊島、犬島、津目島、基島、竹島、小竹島、三郎島、小守島、二股島、新島）^(*)[*] その他19（島7、小島5、此島4、一島、孤島、最遠島）
計	必ずしも島名とはいえない地名等29 特定島名76 その他21

凡例：数字は件数。数字の無いものは1件。

（＊）これらのほか、『続々群書類従』本には「面例御島」なる島名が出てくるが、『日本庶民生活史料集成』本では「面洲御崎」とする。ここでは後者にしたがい、島名としては採らない。

F其沖に松島あり、上に松生て樹間に荒園あり、長事二町
ばかり、昔好事者此州に雉の無事を愁て、試に雲州より
雌雄を渡して此に放つ、一年を経て終に亡と云（同前、
四六五頁下段）

右のうちA〜Dは、いずれも巻一「国代記」に含まれる記
述、E・Fは、巻二・島後周吉郡のうちそれぞれ「上西里」
項と「蛸木浦」項に含まれる記述である。これら六例につい
て、「此州」とする四例（A・C・E・F）とそれ以外（B
「隣州」・D「一州」）とに分けて検討してみよう。
　まず後者から。Bでは、出雲国の刺史（国守）尼子伊予守
は、佐々木一族の棟梁であり隣州の盟主である、というのだ
から、「隣州」というのは「隠岐国に隣接する出雲国」とい
うこととなる。ここでいう「州」は「国」の意である。Dは、
「国代記」に記された戦国期隠岐国をめぐる政治情勢を前提
に理解しなければならない。隠岐を一国支配していた佐々木
為清の死後、実子五郎が幼少のため為清の弟清家が跡を継い
だ。そして清家の子才又郎が毛利元就のもとに質となった。
佐々木家旧臣たちは、同輩であった清家・才又郎に仕える
ことを潔しとせず、幼君五郎を主君として清家・才又郎と対
立した。安芸国にいた才又郎は元就に愁訴して軍勢を借り、

出雲国まで到った。このとき「一州の人」すなわち隠岐国
じゅうの人々が、五郎君が年少であることを良いことに備え
を怠っていたというのである。ところで、引用文中を一瞥す
るだけでも、「芸州」「雲州」「隠州」のように、国単位での
政治動向が記されることに気づく。「一州」は引用文冒頭に
ある「一国」と同義であり、隠岐国のことを指している。こ
こでいう「州」もまた「国」の意である。
　次に、「此州」とする四例（A・C・E・F）を検討して
みよう。Aは、いま議論の焦点となっている部分なので、
いったん保留しておく。Cは、Dに少しだけ先行する時期の
記事である。毛利元就による隠岐国責めの風聞を前に、亡き
主君の子五郎を擁する旧臣たちは、対立する才又郎が元就の
威を借りて「此州」に攻め込んできた場合、自分たちはかつ
ての同輩一族から馬卒扱いを受けることを恐れている。ここ
での「此州」は、「此（この）」が指示する固有名詞が直近部
分には存在しないものの、敢えて文脈から推せば「隠岐国」
となる。Eは、巻二・島後周吉郡のうち「上西里」項に、
「昔鄭交題二古塚一曰」として始まる引用文のなかで現れる。
この引用文中には、「此州」の「此（この）」に対応すべき適
当な固有名詞が存在しない。Fもまた、「此州」の「此（こ
の）」に対応すべき適当な固有名詞が存在しない。仮に

「州」は「島」の意だとして、直近の「松島」が「此州」に該当するとしてみよう。「昔好事者」以下は、「昔ある好事家が、松島に雊がいないことを残念に思って、(繁殖に失敗し)一年後にはいなくなった」となる。しかしながら、島後周吉郡蛸木浦沖合いの松島に雊がいないからといって、隠岐国内の他所から連れてくるのではなく、わざわざ出雲国から雊を連れてくる、とする記述はいささか不自然な話である。「此州」にいないから「雲州(出雲国)」より連れてきた、とする語の釣り合いからすれば、やはりここは「隠州(隠岐国)」とするのが妥当だろう。この「州」は「島」の意とはならない。

右の検討から、C・E・Fには共通する特徴を指摘することができる。「此(この)」なる指示代名詞を受けるはずの固有名詞が、存在しないか、少なくとも直近部分には存在しない、という点である。それはとりわけEの場合に顕著だが、これらの文章が読み手によって内容理解がなされていたはずである。なぜか。それは「此州」なる語は、すべて「隠州視聴合紀」と題された書物のなかで使用されているからである。その全体についてであれ一部についてであれ、そこに記述さ

れているのは「隠州(隠岐国)」についての事象である。そうした了解が前提としてあったからこそ、これら「此州」は、近くにそれを受ける固有名詞が無くても「隠州(隠岐国)」のことを指すと読み手に理解され得たのである。したがってEの該当部分は、「隠岐国の老人のなかには村上天皇の末孫を称して村上某と称するものがある。その理由を問うと、唐橋(唐橋中将・源雅清)の遺腹なのだという」として了解できる。[13]

一方、「島(嶋)」の用例は、必ずしも島名とはいえない地名等に二九例を得るほかは、特定島名として使用される例が大多数(七六例)である。「その他」に分類した二一例も、例外なく「周囲が水によって囲まれた小陸地」(『広辞苑』「島・嶋」項)としての島にかかわる語ばかりである。

ところで「その他」に分類したうち指示語「此」を含む五つの事例について、以下簡単に検討してみよう。

G津戸に渡る半に篷島と云あり、皆大岩なり、昔津戸・蛸木此島をあらそふ、(『続々群書類従』第九、四五〇頁上段、巻二・島後周吉郡「蛸木浦」項)

H海路半を過て大守島と云有、東西三町計、岩間有りて舟を倚す、或は風起潮渦まく時は此島に舟を倚て生を得たる者多し、(同前、四六七頁上段、巻三・島前穏地郡

「津戸」項）

I 河の南に見付嶋と云あり、蓋崎村より入来る船の先づ此嶋を見に依り、（同前、四七四頁上段、巻四・島前知夫郡「知夫郡」項）

J 岸を離れて五町ばかり南の沖に基島あり、廻り十町ばかり、其上に竹を産する故に竹島とも云、西風属しく潮煙常に灌ぎかゝる、此故に竹の色班々として節高からず、葉も又短じ、好事の者此を求る事多し、然ども四面絶壁にして而も林中蛇多し、若此島に至らんと欲者は風浪の穏なるを窺ひ孤舟に乗て岸に至り、（同前、四七七頁下段、巻四・島前知夫郡「知夫湊」項）

G〜Jの「此島（嶋）」は、それぞれG「篷島」・H「大守島」・I「見付嶋」・J「竹島（基島）」を受けていることが明らかである。また前掲Aにある「此二島」が「松島」「竹島」を指すことも明瞭である。したがって「此島（嶋）」「此二島」とする指示語には、先行する部分に固有島名が必ず存在する。

以上、「隠州視聴合紀」における「州」および「島（嶋）」の用例をすべて検討した結果、「隠州視聴合紀」における「州」の用例六六例のうち、保留してあるAを除く六五例が「国」の意で使用されていることが分かった。また先行する

固有島名を再び指示しようとして、指示詞「此」を含む語によって当該の島を再び指示しようとする際には「此島（嶋）」という語を使用していることも指摘した。[14] これは換言すれば、先行する固有島名を再び指示する際に「此州」という語を使用しないということである。

したがって、これらを踏まえるならば、先に保留しておいたAも、「そうであるならば則ち、日本の北西の地は隠岐州（隠岐国）をもって限りとす」としか読みようがない。それは文章構成の上からもそのようにしか読めないし、用語法上の特徴からもそのようにしか読めない。にもかかわらず、Aにおける「此州」だけは「島（嶋）」の意で解釈しなければならない、とするのはあまりにも無理な話であり、恣意的との誹りを免れえない。

二、「此州」を「竹島（鬱陵島）」とする説について

1 「隠州視聴合紀」の読まれ方

「隠州視聴合紀」「国代記」冒頭部分の解釈をめぐる議論は、竹島／独島の帰属をめぐる日韓両政府間の見解往復と関わっ

て展開したこともまた事実である。そこで、これら見解往復のなかで当該史料の解釈をめぐる議論がどのようであったかについて、[塚本孝]による整理を借りながら検討してみよう。

まず、一九五三年七月一三日付（日本政府見解）および同年九月九日付（韓国政府見解）の第一回見解往復のなかでは、当該史料について一切言及がない。次いで、一九五四年二月一〇日付日本政府見解で初めて史料名として「隠州視聴合紀」が挙げられ、これに対する韓国政府見解では「隠州視聴合紀」を「証拠としては無効」と述べるにとどまり、日韓両政府ともこの見解往復時には「隠州視聴合紀」の解釈問題にまでは及んでいない。[15]

一九五六年九月二〇日付日本政府見解において、「『隠州視聴合記』（一六六七年）も、松島（今日の竹島）および竹島（鬱陵島）をもって日本の北西部の限界と見ている。」[塚本孝、五三頁]とする解釈が、日本の北西部の限界として初めて具体的に示された。これに対する韓国政府の反論が、一九五九年一月七日付韓国政府見解中で以下のように展開された。

日本側は、自己の主張を補強するために『隠州視聴合記』を引用したが、その引用が大きな誤読である。この本は、隠州が日本の乾地（西北限界）であるとしているので

ある。その原文を引用すれば、

隠州在北海中　故云隠岐嶋(割注)「按倭訓海中言遠故名与」

南方至雲州美穂関　戌亥間行二日一夜有松島　又一日程有竹島　此二島無人之地　見高麗如自雲州望隠州　然則日本之乾地以此州為限矣

ここでいう松島は独島、竹島は鬱陵島を指しているので、この二島から高麗（韓国）本土を望見する距離関係が、まるで雲州から隠州を望観するのと同じであり、それすなわち、日本の西北部はこの州を限界とするということである。日本側が二島を「日本の北西部の限界」だとしたのは、誤りである。『隠州視聴合記』の記事こそ正当な見解である。[塚本孝、五六頁]

右の韓国政府見解に対して日本政府としての正式の反論はなされず、[16]こののち「隠州視聴合紀」の解釈問題が両国政府間で改めて取り上げられることはなかった。

ところで、右の整理から、「隠州視聴合紀」の記述が二つの側面から読み込まれていることが分かる。（甲）竹島／独島が松島の名で文献に登場する初見史料として、（乙）一七世紀半ば日本における北西方向の境界を指示する史料として、

である。そして、（乙）に関わって「日本之乾地以三此州一為レ
限矣」の解釈が問題となってくるのである。そこで、日韓両
政府間における見解往復に際して「隠州視聴合紀」に言及の
あった一九五四〜五九年より少し幅を広くとって、この史料
がどのように読み込まれてきたかについて、以下年次を追っ
て検討してみよう。

本稿末尾に付した「『隠州視聴合紀（記）』に言及した諸論
稿」は、「隠州視聴合紀（記）」に言及した論稿で管見の限り
で得られたものすべてについて、関連する記述部分を抜粋し
て公表順に並べたものである。

これを通覧すると、（甲）については、一九〇六年の奥原
碧雲から二〇〇一年の慎鏞廈に到るまで、約二〇件見いだせ
る見解のあいだに相違が見られない。「隠州視聴合紀」が、
竹島／独島が松嶋の名で日本側文献に登場する初見史料であ
る、という点については見解が一致しているということであ
る。

これに対し、（乙）に関わっては、様々な点で見解に違い
が見いだせる。それは以下に示す（Ⅰ）と（Ⅱ）の対立見解、
それらから派生する（Ⅰ）と（Ⅱ）"（Ⅱ）の対立見解に整理
することができようかと思う。

（Ⅰ）一七世紀半ばに、日本領の西北限界が鬱陵島（当時
の竹島）と見なされていた。

（Ⅱ）一七世紀半ばに、日本領の西北限界が隠岐国（隠岐
島）と見なされていた。

（Ⅰ）一七世紀半ばに、鬱陵島（竹島）・竹島／独島が日本
領と考えられていた。

（Ⅱ）一七世紀半ばに、鬱陵島（竹島）・竹島／独島は日本
領ではないと考えられていた。

（Ⅱ）"一七世紀半ばに、鬱陵島（竹島）・竹島／独島が朝鮮
領と考えられていた。

（Ⅰ）は、一九〇六年の奥原碧雲、一九五〇年代末〜六〇
年代初めと思われる田川孝三、六八年の大熊良一、九六年の
下條正男、二〇〇〇年の内藤正中、〇四年の下條正男それぞ
れの見解、および一九五六年九月日本政府見解中に見いだ
せる。また（Ⅰ）は、一九五三年の外務省調査局（執筆者は
川上健三）、五四年の黄相基の見解中に見いだせる。

一方、（Ⅱ）は、一九五七年、六五年の黄相基、六九年の
李漢基、七八年の梶村秀樹、八五年の宋炳基、崔爽祐、白忠
鉉、八九年、九一年の慎鏞廈、九六年の李薫、クヮ
ク・チャンコン、金炳烈、二〇〇一年の慎鏞廈それぞれの見

解、および（Ⅰ）は、一九五九年一月韓国政府見解中に見いだせる。また、（Ⅱ）は、一九八五年の宋炳基、白忠鉉、"（Ⅱ）は、一九六五年の黄相基a、八九年、九一年、九六年の慎鏞廈、九六年の李薫、二〇〇一年の慎鏞廈、それぞれの見解中に見いだすことができる。

さて、まず（Ⅱ）では、「此州」を「隠州」と解する論拠がどう説明されているだろうか。「精読すれば…分明だ」［李漢基］とか「文章上も意味上も妥当」［金炳烈］というのは説明不足だとすれば、「この書の主対象である隠州だからだ」［黄相基一九六五b］とか「報告書の主題（隠州視聴合記）であるとともに、冒頭にある「隠州は…」とおしまいあたりの此州の直前に現れる州名を受けて」［クワク・チャンコン］というのが具体的な論拠といえようか。

2　「此州」を「鬱陵島」とする論拠（一）

先述した（Ⅰ）で「此州」を「鬱陵島」と解する論拠は、田川孝三、下條正男、内藤正中の見解中で示される。

まず、田川孝三は「然則日本之乾之地、以二此州一為レ限矣」について、「然則」なる接続詞に注意を喚起しつつ、以下のように述べる。

竹島の地は、是より高麗を見ること恰も雲州より隠州を見るが如くである。上記の如くであるから、すなわち、日本の乾の方の限界は此の州（州はシマの意である）なので、あると釈読しなければならぬ。故に従前の諸書にも地図にも、この意味の如く解して書いて来ているのである。［田川孝三、四二～四三頁］

この史料解釈は、「高麗を見るに雲州より隠州を望むが如し。然らば則ち、日本の乾の地は、此州を以て限となすな」の「高麗を見る」位置について、「この二島（鬱陵島と竹島／独島―引用者）から高麗（韓国）本土を望見する」（註17参照）とした韓国政府見解の誤読に対し、「鬱陵島（竹島）から見て」と訂正するものである。しかしながら、「然則」で挟まれた前後だけを抜き出して読んだために「此州」の主語が「見高麗」の主語と一致すると錯覚し、ために「州」を「島」と読み替えざるをえなくなったのである。ところで右に引用した文中で田川のいう「従前の諸書」「地図」とは、「隠岐国古記」と長久保赤水「日本輿地路程全図」（そのなかの竹島傍注）のことである。これらには確か[18]に竹島（鬱陵島）から朝鮮半島が見えると記されている。しかし、そのことは、「竹島（鬱陵島）と高麗」「出雲と隠岐」

それぞれが互いに視認できる位置関係にあることを示しているだけであって、竹島（鬱陵島）が日本領だなどとはどこにも書いていない。したがって「すなわち、日本の乾の方の限界は此の州（州はシマの意である）なのであると釈読しなければならぬ」などというのは願望をそのまま決意表明したに過ぎないのである。

「州」に「島」の意味があるのは一般論としてはそのとおりである。しかし田川は、「隠州視聴合紀」中に数多くある「州」のうち右の部分だけは「島」と解さねばならないことについて、何らの客観的検討もしておらず、これでは論として成り立ちようがない。

下條正男説は、慎鏞廈・李漢基説に対し、「最も重要な箇所を無視」したり「『隠州視聴合記』から自説に都合のよい箇所だけを抜き出して解釈し、『国代記』の文章全体を読んでいなかった」ために「此州」を「隠州」と誤読したと批判する［下條正男、二〇〇四］。それは具体的には ② を読まずにこの史料を解釈」した［下條正男、二〇〇四］とか「（一）と（七）だけを引用して…反論しているのである」［下條正男二〇〇四・一七〇頁］とする批判である。しかしながら、李漢基・慎鏞廈いずれの史料引用・現代語訳をみても、下條正男の指摘するような過失があるようには読めない。

というのも、第一に、「最も重要な箇所」における論法は、「然則日本之乾地、以此州為限矣」に直接影響を及ぼさないからである。「最も重要な箇所」では、「従是南」「（従是）辰巳」「（従是）未申」「（従是）自子至卯」「（従是）戌亥間」の「隠岐国（隠岐島）から」なる言葉を省略しつつ、ように、「隠岐国（隠岐島）から」なる言葉を省略しつつ、隠岐を基点として四方位を眺めるという観点をとっている。

この「隠岐を基点とする」観点ないし論法が最終一文「然則日本之乾地、以此州為限矣」にまで及ぶのだとすれば、主語の転換は不要である。隠岐を基点とする観点から日本を基点とする観点に主語が転換したから、わざわざ「日本之乾地」と明記したのである。[19]

第二に、「最も重要な箇所」を抜かした史料解釈は、田川孝三にも共通する。最終一文「然則日本之乾地、以此州為限矣」解釈のために田川が必要としたのは「戌亥の間、行くこと二日一夜にして松島あり」以降の部分だけであり、こうした抜粋のしかたは李漢基・慎鏞廈両者とまったく同じである。

ありうるとすれば、それは下條正男が「最も重要な箇所」とする部分のすべてを引用したり釈読したりしていない、という点に求めることはできる。しかしながらそのことは、当該史料とりわけ「然則日本之乾地、以此州為限矣」の解釈に当たって大きな問題ではない。

下條正男説は、結局このところ「見高麗如自雲州望隠岐、然則日本之乾地以此州為限矣」だけを抜き出して読み、誤解した。田川孝三の同じ轍を踏んでいる。先述したように「見高麗如自雲州望隠岐」のどこにも竹島（鬱陵島）とは書いていないばかりか、「隠州視聴合記」すべてを精読してもそうした記述は出てこない。にもかかわらず、「高麗を見ること雲州の隠岐を望むがごとし」は、高麗（朝鮮）を見ている位置は当然日本領と認識しているわけで、竹島、鬱陵島、隠岐島の中で雲州（島根）から隠岐島を見るように朝鮮が見えるのは、鬱陵島だけしかない」［下條正男一九六・六九頁］とか「日本領から高麗（朝鮮）が望めるのは、「国代記」の中では鬱陵島だけである」［下條正男二〇〇四・一七一頁］などとする思いこみである。

そうした思いこみの補強説明として、「隠州視聴合記」が書かれた当時の出雲藩には、竹島（鬱陵島）を日本として認識するだけの事情があった」［下條正男二〇〇四・一七一頁］という。その主たる論拠は、米子の大谷・村川両家が竹島渡海を繰り返していた事実が「隠州視聴合記」に記載されているというところに求められている。

たしかに、大谷・村川両家は、「竹島渡海免許」を受けて、

年に一度、竹島（鬱陵島）へ渡海し、数ヶ月同島に滞留しながら漁業活動を行った。大谷・村川両家は、竹島（鬱陵島）および松島（竹島／独島）を将軍家から拝領したと述べているから、これをもって日本領と認識したと考えがちである。

しかしながら、「竹島渡海免許」は、大谷・村川両家が同業の競合者を排除するために、旗本阿部家を介して得た「渡海免許」であり、したがって竹島（鬱陵島）へ大谷・村川家および同家に雇われた者以外は渡海できなかった。また竹島（鬱陵島）へは毎年一度渡海したのみであって、漁期が終われば鳥取藩領に戻ったから、誰もそこに居住しなかった。こうした状態は、客観的にみたときに「日本領」であったとは言いがたい。

また、少し後のこととなるが、元禄八年（一六九五）一二月、鳥取藩江戸藩邸は老中阿部正武の問いに対し「竹島は因幡・伯耆附属にては無御座候」と述べた。これを受けて翌年正月九日、対馬藩国元家老に対し、「（竹島は）因幡・伯耆江附属と申二而も無之」「日本人居住候か、此方江取候島に候ハ、今更遣しかたき事候得共、左様之証拠等も無之」などと述べた［池内敏二〇〇一・一九〜二〇頁］。すなわち鳥取藩は、竹島（鬱陵島）を鳥取藩領としたことがないと述べ、幕府も自分の領土としたことがないと明言しているのである。

大谷・村川家が竹島（鬱陵島）で排他的に漁業活動をしてき
ただけであって「日本領」ではなく、そのようにも認識され
てはいなかった。

3 「此州」を「鬱陵島」とする論拠（二）

『隠州視聴合紀』の著者が竹島（鬱陵島）を日本領と認識
していたとするもう一つの論拠は、史料中「竹島」に付され
た割注である。そこには、竹島が別名磯竹島と呼ばれる由来
を「神言」の「五十猛」から説明する（磯竹島…按、神言所
謂五十猛獣）が、竹島（鬱陵島）を日本領と認識していなけ
ればこうした記述はありえないという。しかしながら、［史
料二］を掲げた際にも記したように、『隠州視聴合記』の諸
本によって、この按語部分があるものと無いものとがある
（表2も参照）。そうである以上、①斎藤豊仙が当初書き上げ
たものには右の按語がなかったが後に付け加えられた、また
は、②当初は右の按語があったが後に何らかの事情で削除さ
れた、のいずれかとなる。

ところで、西尾市岩瀬文庫史料中に「隠岐国風土記」と題
する冊子がある。これは、宝永六年（一七〇九）に殺人の罪
を犯して隠岐国へ流罪となった京都の医師尾関意仙が、配流
先の隠岐で記した記録である。元文元年（一七三六）に伊勢

神戸の医師のもとに寄せられたものという。その冒頭部分に
以下の記述（［史料二］）があるが、「隠州視聴合記」国代記
を踏まえた記述であることは［史料二］と比較すれば一目瞭
然である。

［史料二］
隠州者在北海中故名隠岐嶋矣、其在異地言島前也、凡二郡、
知夫郡・海部郡郡村数十三属焉、其位震地言嶋後、凡二郡周吉
郡・穏地郡村数五十三属焉、其府者周吉郡南岸西郷豊崎也、
従是離之方至出雲国海上三十五里、至同積積浦・北浦十
八里、至長門下関百里、巽之方至伯州赤崎四十里、艮之方至
若州小浜百二十里、自子至卯無可往地、乾之間二昼一夜走而
有松嶋、又一昼走有竹嶋、俗云磯竹嶋、此二島無人之地也、
或云、春夏秋之間朝鮮人来漁蚫・海鹿之類乎、寛文年中□者
自隠州往滞舟而漁採桐・梅檀・竹芳之類帰也、近年闕其、従
竹嶋見高麗如自雲州望隠州、然則日本之乾地、以此州為限矣、

右史料中の傍線部分を［史料二］の当該部分「戌亥間行二
日一夜有二松島一、又一日程有二竹島一（割注）「俗言二磯竹島
一、多二竹・魚・海鹿一（「、按、神言所謂五十猛獣）、此二
島無人之地」と対比すれば、いま問題とする按語部分の無

表2　「磯竹島」割注・按語部分の異同

	按語部分なし	按語部分あり		書写年代
		神書	神言	
続々群書類従	○			
日本庶民生活史料集成	○			
鶴舞図書館・河村文庫		○		1740年代半ば以後か(*1)
西尾市岩瀬文庫		○		宝暦元年（1751）以後(*2)
ソウル大図書館			○	享和二年（1802）(*3)

（＊1）本冊子中に「河邨蔵書」印（河村秀根蔵書印）があり、本冊子が河村秀根による集書の一部であることが分かる。秀根の生存したのは1719-92年であり、学問を学んだのが20代の頃であったこと（『国史大辞典』「河村秀根」項）から推測。

（＊2）巻末に「南窓随筆抄　焼火権現」が収録され、その記述中に「宝暦元年三月焼失」とする記載があることから。

（＊3）奥書に享和二年に筆写したことが明記されている。

いことが分かる。

　また、後掲【史料三】として「隠岐古記集」（一八二三年成立）を掲げたが、ここでは、竹島を磯竹島とも呼称する理由が「其嶋の丑ノ方に弓嵩有と見ゆ、彼嵩を呼んて当地の人磯嵩嶋と号しならんか」（傍線部ウ）と説明される。本書は「当国にて古ヨリ磯竹と云伝へあり、（割注）「隠州視聴合記」をも参照しつつ、（視聴合記）記に見へたり」とするから、磯竹島なる呼称の由来を考証しつつ、そこには「五十猛」の話は引用されない。

　これらからすれば、「隠岐国風土記」「隠岐古記集」成立の時点では「隠州視聴合記」の当該部分に「五十猛」に関わる按語が書かれていなかったか、もしくは書かれていたが「隠岐国風土記」「隠岐古記集」の著者がその説を採用しなかったか、のいずれかとなる。とすれば、問題の按語部分は、一六六七年当時から書かれていた斎藤豊仙の見解と見るのは困難に思えるし、仮に一六六七年当時に書かれていたとして、後世の人がその説を採用しなかった事実は重い。いずれにしても問題の按語部分を根拠にして、当時隠岐国では竹島（鬱陵島）を日本領と見ていた、と結論づけるのは難しい。

　ところで、内藤正中もまた、「竹島（鬱陵島）を日本の乾地（西北境）と思って記述したことは当然と見なければならな

い」とし、「隠岐古記集」を援用して以下のように述べる。

なお、一八二三年（文政六）の大西教保による『隠岐古記集』では、「此島より朝鮮を望免は隠州より雲州を見るより猶遠して、今は朝鮮人来て住すと言ふ」と記し、「此島」が竹島（鬱陵島）であることを明らかにしている。本書は前述『隠州視聴合紀』を底本にして、さらに増補したものといわれている以上、『隠州視聴合紀』における「日本乾地」は竹島（鬱陵島）となる。[内藤正中、一二二頁]

さて、『隠州視聴合紀・国代記』冒頭部分を[史料二]より再掲して[史料四]として併記し、両書の異同を検討してみたい。

[史料三]

歴代史を考るにa日本の乾地此国を以て限りとする也、b雲州三保関ヨリ三拾五里、c震地に在る島後といふ、周吉郡・越智郡焉に属す、其の南岸をd西郷といふ、国中の府とす、東は大久村ヨリ西は里三拾町、北は西村より南は今津村迄長五里、e是ヨリ坤地に位するを嶋前といふ、知

夫里郡・海士郡焉に属す、所謂三つに分る 「知夫里郡二嶋、海士郡壱嶋」、別府村を以て府とす、其南は知夫里村より北は宇賀村・冠島之磯迄四里余長とす、東は布施村ヨリ西は美田村船越の西の出島迄三里余とす、島之物周里拾六里程、又f未申ノ方五拾八里にして石州温泉津に至る、g辰巳ノ方四拾里伯州赤碕あり、ア卯方凡百里にして若州小浜に至り、丑寅ノ方凡三拾里余能州に当る、h亥ノ方四十余里にして松前あり、周り凡壱里程にして生木なき岩嶋といふ、i又酉ノ方七十余里余に竹嶋〔あり、古より是を磯竹島〕といひ伝ふj竹木繁茂して大島の由、k是より朝鮮を望めは隠州より雲州を見るより尚近しと云、イ今は朝鮮人来住すと云々、愚諸国の船人に問尋するに方角誠に然り、秋清天北風の日に大満寺山の頂上ヨリ望み見は、松島は遥か見へんといふ、ウ竹島は朝鮮の池山に懐かれ遠く望めは朝鮮地と見ゆる由、愚按、当国より古ヨリ磯竹と云伝へあり、「視聴合記に見へたり」今や朝鮮の図面を見るに、彼国市師より寅卯ノ方、亦対馬国豊浦より子ノ方に当りて鬱陵嶋といふもあり、其嶋の丑ノ方に弓嵩とて高山有と見ゆ、彼嵩を呼んで当地の人磯嵩嶋と号しならんか、当国に百里の内外に彼二嶋より外見へさる由なり、人の住居するも近頃にてハ有まじ、

【史料四】

隱州在二北海中一 故隱岐嶋（割注）「按、倭訓海中言二遠幾一、故名歟」、e′其在二巽地一言二島前一也、知夫郡・海部郡属レ焉、c′其位二震地一言二島後一、周吉郡・穩地郡属レ焉、d′其府者周吉郡南岸西郷豊崎也、従レ是南至二b′雲州美穗関二三十五里、g′辰巳至二伯州赤碕浦二四十里、f′未申至二石州温泉津一五十八里、自レ子至レ卯無二可レ往地一、h′戌亥間行二日一夜有二松島一、i′又一日程有二竹島一（割注）「俗言二磯竹島一、j′多二竹・魚・海鹿一、此二一島無レ人之地、k′見二高麗一如レ自二雲州一望二隱岐上、然則a′日本之乾之地、以二此州一為レ限矣、

傍線部分（aとa′～kとk′）が「隱岐古記集」「隱州視聴合紀」の両史料にほぼ共通する記述として対応関係が認められる部分である。傍線の付されていない箇所との関連性があったり、波線部ア・イには一六六〇年代から一八二〇年のあいだにかけて起こった出来事にもとづく知見の拡大が反映していると思われるから、「隱岐古記集」は、たしかに「隱州視聴合紀」を踏まえて増補されたものといえる。そうした場合、a「日本の乾地此此国を以て限りとする也」とa′「日本之乾之地、以二此州一為レ限矣」との対応関係は看過すべきではない。こ

こには、「隱州視聴合紀」の解釈をめぐって問題となっている「此州」とは「此国（隱岐国）」のことであることが明示され、それが「日本之乾地」だと明示されている。「隱岐古記集」と「隱州視聴合紀」を対比した場合、内藤のいうような「日本乾地」は竹島（鬱陵島）となる」という結論は決して得られないのである。

おわりに

「史料はやはり一部を読んで解釈するのではなく、全体をみて読むべきではなかろうか」「もう少し慎重に史料を読むべきではなかろうか」【下條正男一九六・七〇頁上段】というのは同感である。「隱州視聴合紀」から自説に都合のよい箇所だけを抜き出して解釈し、「国代記」の文章全体を読んでいなかった」というのではいけない【下條正男二〇〇四・一六八頁】、というのもその通りである。本稿ではそうした誤りを排するためにも、極力「隱州視聴合紀」を丁寧に読み込んでみたつもりである。

さて、「隱州視聴合紀」は、従来いわれてきたような、竹島／独島がかつて松島と呼ばれていたことを示す最古の文献

史料というわけではない。一六五〇年代初頭のものと推測される大谷家文書のなかに、「松島」なる島名で竹島/独島が登場するからである［池内敏一九九九・三七頁］。また、この史料をもって、一六六〇年代に竹島/独島が日本領と認識されていたとすることはできないことについては先に述べた。

一方、この史料をもって、竹島/独島が当時の日本の版図から外れたものと認識されていたとする（先に整理した〝(Ⅱ)の見解〟）のは妥当だとしても、それがすなわち朝鮮領だ〝(Ⅱ)〟ということにはならない。〝(Ⅱ)〟は、文意を逸脱した無理な解釈である。したがってこの「隠州視聴合紀」なる史料は、竹島/独島の帰属を示す歴史的根拠として使用することは日韓いずれの側にとっても適当ではなく、そうした議論の現場から退くべきものなのである。

【註】

(1) 解題によれば、ここに収録されたものは、一写本を翻刻した出雲文庫刊行会本（一九一四年）を底本とし、西郷町服部家蔵本（写本）を翻刻した隠岐郷土研究会刊行会本（一九六三年）を参考本とし、西郷町佐々木章家伝来本（写本）をもって校訂したものという。

(2) 『日本庶民生活史料集成』本では構成が少し異なり、巻四のうち、「名所和歌」が文覚論のうしろに来る。また、嶋後・嶋前を描いた地図一葉が付されている。

(3) 『続々群書類従』本と、『日本庶民生活史料集成』本との差異については註（二）以下で触れる。これらのほかにもうひとつソウル大学校付属図書館に所蔵された「隠州視聴合記」（以下ソウル大本と表記する）をも参照し、先の二本にはなく、ソウル大本にのみある語句については〔 〕書きして示した。また、挿図（嶋後・嶋前の地図）に付された地名や送りがなの振り方の違いなど、いちいち触れずに割愛した。

なお、ソウル大本は、表紙見返し部分に「京城帝国大学図書章」（朱印）があり、第一丁表に「肱野蔵書」（朱印）がある。請求記号は4710－172。巻末に異筆で「隠州視聴合記目録之書、愚何幸見之、仍為廻嶋使理令臨写焉、勿論文字不正其佚而、嶋前別府署於小各亭、皆享和二年壬戌冬陽復之月某日也」とあり、署名を「井専方」とし、「井専方印」「林亭」二つの朱印（書き印）がある。

(4) 川上健三『竹島の歴史地理学的研究』五〇頁で引用する『隠州視聴合記』では、「故」と「隠岐嶋」のあいだに「云」が挿入される。川上は『続々群書類従』地理部第九から史料引用したとする（川上著書六五頁・注（一九））が、同史料は本稿で引用した如くであり、「云」字はない。『日本庶民生活史料集成』本でも同様。川上の注記によれば、「なお内閣文庫には、『隠州視聴合記』写本もある」とするから、あるいは川上の典拠はこちらであったかもしれない。とした場合、それはソウル大本と類似している。

『隠州視聴合記』を川上健三著書から再引用する類似した事例が多

いので、念のため付記しておく。

(5)　『日本庶民生活史料集成』本では、この割注最後の「名歟」を本文とする。またソウル大本では「歟」ではなく「與（与）」とする。

(6)　「震」字は、『続々群書類従』本では「霊」とする。島前を巽地とするのに対応する文言中にあるところからすれば、『日本庶民生活史料集成』本にある「震」字の方がふさわしい。なお、隠岐嶋のうち島後が震（東の方角）に位置するというのはともかく、島前が巽（南東の方角）に位置するというのは実際の位置関係（南西）からすると疑問が残るが、この点については当面保留しておく。

(7)　川上著書で引用する『隠州視聴合紀』も〔　〕に該当する部分があるが、「神言」ではなくて「神書」とする。註（4）参照のこと。

(8)　「雲州」は、『続々群書類従』本では「雲岐」とする。管見の限りでは、「隠岐」を「岐」の字で略した例はなく、また「雲岐（出雲・隠岐）」から隠岐を望むとするのは文意として通らない。したがってここでは『日本庶民生活史料集成』本にしたがう。

(9)　「隠岐」を、ソウル大本では「隠州」とする。

(10)　「頭」字は、『続々群書類従』本では「領」とする。

(11)　田川孝三のこの一文は、一九八八年発行の『東洋文庫書報』二〇号に収載された論文「竹島領有に関する歴史的考察」によって読みうるが、当該論文が作成された時期ははるかに遡るだろう。というのも、この論文は、田川孝三が一九八一年一〇月に没したのち、「未公表論文の中から一篇を選び」、『東洋文庫書報』に掲載されたものだからである。ところで、論文中に以下のような記述が見える。

最近、韓国が提示してきた同国政府の竹島に関する見解は、専らこれ迄のわが国政府の見解に対する反論に終始しており、従来よりの彼の見解の一部を繰返えし主張しているにすぎない。…（中略）…以下、彼が主張を批判しつつ、所見を述べよう（六頁）

韓国の見解において、従前わが国が重要な資料の一として引用してきた隠州視聴合記（寛文七年、一六六七年自序）の記事について、わが方の釈読は誤れるものなりと論じている（四一頁）

こうした記述と、竹島問題に関わる日韓両政府の見解往復における「隠州視聴合紀」関連記事を〔塚本孝〕によって検討すると、おおむね一九五六年九月二〇日付日本政府見解と、それに対する一九五九年一月七日付韓国政府見解のあたりに符合する内容が見いだせる。したがって、田川孝三の論は、一九六〇年ころには形作られていたとみることができる。

(12)　下條正男は「「州」には「島」の意味があり、隠岐島を隠州とするように「此の州」を鬱陵島のこととしても問題はないのである。現に李瀷も『星湖僿説類選』の中で、安龍福の功で鬱陵島が朝鮮に復したことを「一州の土を復す」と記しているからだ。」〔下條正男一九九六、七〇頁〕と述べる。なお、ここで「隠岐島を隠州とするように」という

のは誤解である。「隠岐国」を「隠州」とするのであって、「隠岐島」を「隠州」とするのではない。こう言うと、「国代記」冒頭部分の「隠州在二北海中一、故隠岐嶋」を取り上げて、「州」を「島（嶋）」と読み替えているではないかとする反論が直ちに予想されるが、この反論は成り立たない。冒頭部分以下数行を、いま論証に不要な割注部分を省いて再掲する。

隠州在二北海中一、故隠岐嶋、其、在二巽地一、言二島前一也、知夫郡・海部郡属レ焉、其、位二震地一、言二島後一、周吉郡・穏地郡属レ焉、其府者周吉郡南岸西郷豊崎也、（以下略）

右に見るように「隠州在二北海中一、故隠岐嶋」に引き続く数行の間に「其（その）」なる指示代名詞が三ヶ所（傍線部分①～③）現れる。文脈からいって①～③はいずれも先行する同一の固有名詞を受けていると考えざるをえない。そしてこれに該当する固有名詞は「隠州」ないしは「隠岐嶋」のいずれかしかありえない。①・②については、「隠州」「隠岐嶋」いずれを宛てても構わない。しかしながら③に「隠岐嶋」を宛てることはできない。「府」というのは「国府」のことだからである。こうして③は「隠岐国」の意である。したがって、右の部分にあっても、「州」は「島（嶋）」と読み換えることはできない。

（13）「上西里」項は、左遷されて隠岐に到った唐橋中将（源雅清）が、はじめ島前の布施村におり、のち島後上西里に移り住み、亡くなったという逸話を記す。

（14）このほか、以下に示すように「此」一文字で先行する固有島名を受ける事例も散見される。「此」「従レ是して篷島と号す、今俗此を前平島と号するは…」（『続々群書類従』第九、四六六頁上段）、「東北の海中に小竹島あり、此より海部の崎村に渡ること海路一里語町」（同前、四七七頁下段）、「又北に二股島二并びて大岩の出たるあり、此を新島と云」（同前、四八〇頁下段）

（15）一九五四年二月一〇日付・日本政府見解のうち関連する部分は以下の通り。「竹島は、古く松島の名において日本人に知られ、日本領土の一部として考えられ、また日本人によって航海上または漁業上利用されていた。ことに徳川三代将軍家光時代、幕府から米子の町人大谷、村川両家に対して竹島の支配が許され、鬱陵島に渡航の際には常にこの島が中継基地として利用されるとともに、同島において漁猟も行われていた。右に関する文献としては、寛文七年（一六六七）の出雲藩士斎藤某編『隠州視聴合記』、延宝九年（天和元年＝一六八一）の大谷九右衛門勝信手記などがあり、地図としては、享保年中（一七二〇年代）の鳥取藩主池田家旧蔵「竹島図」、安永四年（一七七五）の長久保赤水の「日本輿地路程全図」などがある。」塚本孝・六〇頁。一方、同年九月二五日付・韓国政府見解中の該当する部分は以下の通り。「日本政府は独島領有権に関する証拠文書として以下の通り隠州視聴合記（一六六七）と大谷九右衛門手

記（一六八一年）をあげているが、これらの文書は日本の鬱陵島水域侵略時代（一六一四年から一六九七年まで）に書かれたものであるから、韓国政府は、これを証拠として無効であるとみなす。［塚本孝・五四頁］

(16) 塚本孝はこの韓国政府見解について、「日本政府は、この批判に直接答えていない」とする注を付している。

(17) もっともこれらの見解も、厳密に言えば、日本政府見解が日本の北西部の限界を「鬱陵島と今日の竹島」の両方に置くのに対し、それ以外の見解はそれを鬱陵島だけに置いている、という違いがある。ここで、「松島（今日の竹島）および竹島（鬱陵島）をもって日本の北西部の限界と見ている」という日本政府の見解は、「此州」の「此」が単数を受けるべき指示代名詞であるにもかかわらず、複数の名詞を受けると解したことからも、明らかな誤読である。なお、この日本政府見解に対する韓国政府見解が「この二島から高麗（韓国）本土を望見する距離関係が」と反論するのも、右の誤読に引きずられた誤読である。

(18) 「…竹島あり、古より是を磯竹島と伝う。竹木繁茂して大島の由、是より朝鮮を望めば隠州より雲州を見るより尚近し、…」（「隠岐国古記」、［田川孝三・四一頁］）「見高麗猶雲州望隠州、一曰磯竹島」（「日本輿地路程全図」、［田川孝三・四二頁］）

(19) 「江戸（東京）をその中心に据えれば隠岐島は西にあたる」から隠岐島が日本の西北とする表現は不適当だともいう［下條正男一九九六・七〇頁］。江戸時代当時の感覚で

いえば、江戸（ないし京都）から西方向へ伯耆国米子へゆき（ないしは播磨国姫路まで西方向に進み、そこから北西方向に伯耆国米子へ行く）、そこから北へ向かって三保関を経て隠岐島へ進むのだから、「西北」と感じるのが妥当なのである。また、ふつう江戸から見て西方向といえば長崎をいう。長崎との対比からしても隠岐島は西北とならざるをえない。

(20) 異国渡海朱印状をもって渡航した朱印船の人々が赴いた東南アジア各地が、当時、日本領土になったとは思えない。そこへ居住して日本町をなしても、そこは日本領とはいえなかった。まして、居住の実態もなく、大谷・村川両家に雇われない限り渡航できないような土地が、当時「日本領」と考えられていたとはとても考えられない。しかも「竹島渡海免許」は異国渡海朱印状とは性格が異なり、寛永二年（一六二五）一回切りの発行であり、幕府は毎年の渡航をきちんと把握しきっていたわけではなかった［池内敏一九九九］ばかりか、竹島（鬱陵島）の存在すら十分に掌握できていなかった［池内敏二〇〇一］。

(21) いわゆる元禄竹島一件も、領土問題が争われたわけではなかった。大谷・村川両家が求めたのは竹島（鬱陵島）における漁業権の確保であり、彼らが「日本領」の維持を訴えたわけではなかった。また交渉を委ねられた対馬藩も、当初は領土問題として争うつもりではなかった。朝鮮政府側が鬱陵島を朝鮮領と明示するよう求める過程で、この交渉が領土問題の様相を帯びることとなっ

(22) たまでである［池内敏二〇〇二］。

本稿では、大韓民国国史編纂委員会収集史料に含まれる「隠岐古記集」を翻刻掲載した。同史料は一九七〇年代に姜萬吉氏によって収集されたものというが、史料採訪地・典拠等の記載がない。そこで、隠岐郷土研究会編『隠岐島史料』近世編下に収載された「隠岐古記集」と校合した。両史料は概ね一致するが、『隠岐島史料』本が、「里」を「厘」と翻刻するなど、文脈に影響を与えない小さな違いは多数ある。また、大きく異なる点については、［ ］で補った部分が一ヶ所、［イ］として異同表記したものが三ヶ所ある。

(23) 享保二〇年（一七三五）、隠岐島後の四人乗りの船が、商売のために越前へ行き、隠岐へ戻る途上で漂流して朝鮮半島に至った事例がある［松田甲］。この事例からすれば、少なくとも一八世紀初めには、隠岐から若狭から越前・能登あたりまでを往来するようになっており、「隠州視聴合紀」では「往くべき地無し」とされていた東～北方向についての知見が拡大してきたことが、波線部アの記述につながっていよう。また、一七世紀末に生じた元禄竹島一件が、波線部イの記述につながっているだろう。

【参考史料・文献】

『続々群書類従』第九、国書刊行会、一九〇六年

『日本庶民生活史料集成』第二十巻、三一書房、一九七二年

池内敏「竹島渡海と鳥取藩」、『鳥取地域史研究』一、一九九九年

〃「竹島一件の再検討」、『名古屋大学文学部研究論集』〈史学四七〉、二〇〇一年

李漢基『韓国の領土』、ソウル大学校出版部、一九六九年

李薫「朝鮮後期の独島領有争い」、『独島と対馬島』、韓日関係史研究会、一九九六年

梶村秀樹「竹島＝独島問題と日本国家」、『朝鮮研究』一八二、一九七八年

外務省条約局「竹島」『竹島の領有』、一九五三年

奥原碧雲『竹島沿革考』、『歴史地理』八巻六号、一九〇六年

大熊良一『竹島史稿』、原書房、一九六八年

〃「日本の土地とする主張は膨張・植民主義の所産」、『新東亜』四三九号、一九九六年四月

川上健三『竹島の歴史地理学的研究』、古今書院、一九六六年

クァク・チャンコン「独島領有権論争はもう終わった」、『韓国論壇』一九九六年九月号

金炳烈「証拠を無視してはならない」、『韓国論壇』一九九六年一月号

下條正男「竹島問題考」、『現代コリア』三六二、一九九六年

〃「竹島問題の現代的課題」、『国際開発学研究』第二巻一号、二〇〇〇年

〃「竹島は日韓どちらのものか」、文春新書三七七、二〇〇四年

慎鏞廈「朝鮮王朝の独島領有と日本帝国主義の独島侵略」、『韓国独立運動史研究』三、一九八九年

〃「独島主権は死活の民族問題である」、『新東亜』四三九号、一九九六年四月a

「独島の民族領土史研究」、知識産業社、一九九六年b

『独島、大切な韓国領土』、知識産業社、一九九六年c

『独島領有権に対する日本政府批判』、ソウル大学校出版部、二〇〇一年

『韓国と日本の独島領有権論争』、漢陽大学校出版部、二〇〇三年

〃

宋炳基『欝陵島・独島領有の歴史的背景』、『独島研究』、韓国近代史資料研究協議会、一九八五年

田川孝三「竹島領有に関する歴史的考察」、『東洋文庫書報』二〇、一九八八年

田村清三郎『島根県竹島の新研究』、報光社、一九六五年

塚本孝「竹島領有権をめぐる日韓両国政府の見解（資料）」、「レファレンス」六一七、二〇〇二年

崔奭祐「外国の文献に現れた独島」、『独島研究』、韓国近代史料研究協議会、一九八五年

内藤正中『竹島（欝陵嶋）をめぐる日朝関係史』、多賀出版、二〇〇〇年

中村栄孝「磯竹島」（欝陵島）についての覚書」、『日本歴史』一五八、一九六一年（のち、同『日鮮関係史の研究』下、吉川弘文館、一九六九年

河錬洙「竹島紛争」再考」、『龍谷法学』三二巻二号、一九九九年

黄相基「独島問題研究」、ソウル大学校大学院法学科碩士論文、

一九五四年

〃　「独島領有権解説」、『東亜日報』、一九五七年二月二八日～三月五日

〃　「独島問題研究」、『独島』、大韓公論社、一九六五年a

『独島領有権解説』、勤労学生社、一九六五年（再版）b

白忠鉉「国際法上からみた独島紛争」、『独島研究』、韓国近代史資料研究協議会、一九八五年

堀和生「一九〇五年日本の竹島領土編入」、『朝鮮史研究会論文集』二四、一九八七年

松田甲「享保乙卯日本人の朝鮮漂流記」、『日鮮史話』第五編、朝鮮総督府、一九二九年

付録　「隠州視聴合紀（記）」に言及した諸論稿

一九〇六年
【奥原碧雲】

「この岩嶼のはじめて記録に見えたるは、隠岐視聴合記とす（九頁）として『国代記』冒頭の地理的特性を述べた部分を史料引用【甲】

隠州視聴合記に欝陵島即ち竹島を以て無人島にして、日本之乾之地以ニ此州一為ニ限矣とあるを見れば、…（中略）…同書の編者はこの島を以て日本海西北に於ける我領土の極点となせり（一九頁）（乙）

一九五三年八月

【外務省条約局】

今日の竹島はその当時は松島として知られていた。これを文献について見るに、寛文七年（一六六七年）の出雲藩士斉藤某の『隠州視聴合紀』巻一、国代記の部に「隠州在二北海中一故隠岐嶋…戌亥間行二日一夜有二松島一又一日程有二竹島一［割註］」「俗言磯竹島多竹有海鹿、此二島無レ人之地見二高麗一、如下自二雲州一望二隠岐上一、然則日本之乾地以二此州一為レ限矣」とあるのをもって嚆矢とするものの如くである（九頁）【甲】

寛文七年（一六六七年）の『隠州視聴合紀』や延宝九年（一六八一年）の大谷九右衛門勝信の請書等によると、この松島（今の竹島）についてはもちろん竹島（欝陵島）までも日本領土の一部と見做していることが注目される（四七頁）【乙】

一九五四年十二月

【黄相基】

一六六七年寛文七年、斎藤弗緩は隠州視聴合紀を書いたという。文献の第一面には次のような文句が書いてある。「戌亥間行二日一夜有松島　又一日程有竹島（俗云磯竹島多竹海藻）此二島無人之地見高麗如雲州望隠州　然則　日本之乾以此州為限」だという。すなわち日本之乾如雲州望隠州　と松島（独島）が日本の領土だという意味である。（三一～三三頁「出漁時代の日本側文献」項）【乙】

一九五七年三月一日

【黄相基】

しかし隠州視聴合記には次のように書いてある。『戌亥之間行二

日一夜　有松島　又一日程有竹島（俗言磯竹魚海按神言五十猛欤）此二島無人之地　見高麗如雲州望隠州　然則日本之乾地以此州為限矣』この文章の意味は『松島と竹島が無人島であり、竹島から高麗を眺めるのは雲州から隠州を眺めるのと同じである、そういうわけで、日本の限界は此州に限る』ということである。すなわち此州というのは隠州である隠岐島のことを言っているのだが、日本人たちはいまも此州というのは竹島と松島だと解釈しており、外交覚書に引用している（『東亜日報』一九五七年三月一日付、連載第二回記事）。【乙】

一九五〇年代末～六〇年代初

【田川孝三】

韓国の見解において、従前わが国が重要な資料の一として引用してきた隠州視聴合記（寛文七年、一六六七年自序）の記事について、わが方の釈読は誤れるものなりと論じている。即ち逆にこの記事は隠岐を以て日本西北の限界とし、竹島・松島を朝鮮領としたものと解することこそ正しいと反論しているのである。本書問題の記事は

隠州在北海中、故云隠岐嶋…従是、南至雲州美穂関三十五里、辰巳至伯州赤碕浦四十里、未申至石州温泉津五十八里、子至卯、無可往地、戌亥間行二日一夜有松島、又一日程有竹島、俗言磯竹魚海鹿、此二島無人之地、見高麗如自雲州望隠州、然則日本之乾地、以此州為限矣

即ち隠岐の島より東西南北、各方向に従ってその至る地を一応説明したものである。之に倣って記述した隠岐国記（享保五、一七二〇年藪屋比昆編）には、

島の惣廻り十六里、又未申の方五十八里にして石州温泉津に至り、辰巳の方四十里伯州赤碕あり、卯の方凡百里にして若州小浜に至り、丑寅の方凡百三十里余能州に当る、亥の方四十余里にして松島あり、周り一里程にして生木なき岩島という。また西の方七十余里にして竹島あり、古より是を磯竹島と伝う。竹木繁茂して大島にして竹島あり、是より朝鮮を望めば隠州より雲州を見るより尚近し、今朝鮮人来りて住す

とある。是は、前記隠州視聴合記に倣うのみならず、当時の船人にその見聞をききて書きたしたものである。所で合記の問題の条は如何によむべきであろうか。

戊亥の間、行くこと二日一夜にして松島あり、又一日にして竹島あり、…此二島は無人の地なり、高麗を見るに雲州より隠州を望むが如し。然らば則ち、日本の乾の地は、此州を以て限となすなり

とよむべきであろう。高麗を見るに雲州より隠州を望むが如しというのは、竹島と高麗本土との距離が、雲州隠州間の距離と相似ていることをいったものである。即ち「地」と「見」の間に「自竹島」の三字を補えば更に判然となるのである。「此二島無人之地」の七字は、その上を受けて説明したものに過ぎず、「見高麗」以下の主格ではない。又韓国の主張するごとく、二島より高麗を見るに云々とすることは、「如自雲州望隠州」の説明が当たらざるものとなり意味をなさず、極めて無理な解釈である。従って上掲、隠岐国古記にも

竹島といひ伝う、竹木繁茂して大島の由、是より朝鮮を望めば隠州より雲州を見るより尚近し

と補い記しているのである。又長久保赤水の日本輿地路程全図(安永四年、一七七五)以下、江戸時代に刊行された同系統の諸地図には、松島、竹島を図し、竹島の傍註に

見高麗猶雲州望隠州　一日磯竹島

と記しているのである。しかも注目すべきは

…見高麗、如自雲州望隠州、然則日本之乾地、以此州為限矣

とある「然則」の二字である。竹島の地は、是より高麗を見ること恰も雲州より隠州を見るが如くである。すなわち、日本の乾の方の限界は此の州(州はシマの意である)なのであるから、この意味の如く釈読しなければならぬ。故に従前の諸書にも地図にも、この意味の如く解して書かれた記事の意を枉げて解釈しようとするもので、我田に水を引くものというべきである。

[田川孝三、一九八八・四二~四三頁]

一九六一年
【中村栄孝】
「文献の上で、この島(竹島／独島のこと、引用者注)について知り得るのは」(二二頁)として「隠州視聴合紀」「国代記」冒頭の一節を引用(甲)

一九六五年
【黄相基a】
寛文七年(一六六七年)斉藤豊緩の著書隠洲視聴合紀には鬱陵島を「竹島」とし独島は「松島」と称している(二二八頁)(甲)

この合紀（隠州視聴合紀のこと、引用者注）は斉藤弗綬が記述したのであって、戌亥のあいだを行くこと二日一夜にして松島があり、また一日ほど行くと竹島がある。此二島は無人之地である。高麗を見ることはちょうど雲州地方から隠州を眺めることと同じである。だから日本の境界は此州をして限るのであり、竹島（鬱陵島）と松島（独島）が朝鮮領土だということを記述しているのであり、竹島（鬱陵島）と松島（独島）が朝鮮領土だということを言っているにもかかわらず、日本政府は日本領土として記述したもののように誤解しているようだ（二二八頁）（乙）

【黄相基b】

すなわち鬱陵島（竹島）と独島（松島）のこの記事は、文章の脈絡がたいへん模糊としているが、「見高麗如雲州望隠州」というのは、おのおのその本土との距離の近さを意味しているのであり、すなわち隠州は雲州から近く、いわゆる（鬱陵島）（竹島）（松島）独島の二島は高麗すなわち朝鮮に近いということである。とすれば、その次にある「然則日本之乾之地以此州為限矣」というのは、すなわち日本の乾西北界が隠州だ、と解釈せざるをえない。なぜならばいわゆる「此州」というのは、この書の主対象である隠州であるからだ。そうしたゆえに、隠州視聴合紀の第一面にある隠州の地図上には竹島と松島を朝鮮の領土として表示してあるのだ。とすれば、竹島と松島が韓国領土であることは再言を要しない。（四一～四二頁）（乙）

【田村清三郎】

松島の名が最も古く記録せられたものに、松江藩士の編にかかる寛文七年（一六六七）の隠州視聴合記がある。本書は、隠岐島において、著者が自ら視察したまたは聴いたものを記録したものであり、大谷村川両氏の竹島渡海の最盛期の著であることは貴重なものといわなければならない。（七頁）（甲）

一九六六年
【川上健三】

この「松島」の名が、竹島（鬱陵島）とともに文献に現れるようになったのは、出雲藩士斉藤豊仙が寛文七年（一六六七）に編さんした「隠州視聴合記」巻一、国代記の部に、次の通り記されているのがその嚆矢であるといわれる。

「隠州在北海中、故云隠岐嶋。…戌亥間行二日一夜有松島、又一日程有竹島。〔割註〕俗言磯竹島、多竹魚海鹿、按神書所謂五十猛嶼、此二島無人之地、見高麗如自雲州望隠州、然則日本之乾地以此州為限矣」（五〇頁）（甲）

一九六八年
【大熊良一】

竹島の沿革について諸学者や研究者がつねに引用するものは寛文七年（一六六七）に出版された「隠州視聴合記」という一種の地方誌である。…この「隠州視聴合記」の巻一の国代記の章において、問題のこんにちの竹島が記述されている。（甲）…すなわち、この「視聴合記」には隠岐島を中心にして方角が示されているが、「戌亥（西北）の間行くこと二日一夜にして松島（いまの竹島…注）あり、

又一日程にして竹島〈磯竹島＝鬱陵島…注〉あり」と記述されている。そしてこの竹島はこんにちの鬱陵島であり、これが国の境であると編者は述べている。（一五～一六頁）（乙）

一九六九年

【李漢基】

また日本側記録のひとつである「隠州視聴合記」（一六六七年）には、竹島（鬱陵島）および松島（独島）が日本西北部の限界だという文句があると主張し、またこの文句を援用するのが日本の常例となっている。隠州視聴合記は隠州郡隠岐島に関する記事であり、これを精読すれば隠州が日本の乾地（西北界）となっているということは分明だが、日本側は前記したように鬱陵島と独島がその西北限界だと誤読しているのである。その原文を引用すれば、

「隠州在北海中　故云隠岐嶋　按倭訓海中　言遠故名與　南方至雲州美穂関…戌亥間行二日一夜有松島　又一日程有竹島　此二島無人之地　見高麗　如自雲州望隠州　然則　日本之乾地以此州為限矣」

ここにいわゆる松島はすなわち独島を、竹島はすなわち鬱陵島を指しているのであって、「此二島」から高麗（韓国）本土を望見する距離関係が、ちょうど雲州から隠州を望見するのと同様であり、したがって日本の西北部は此州をもって限界とするということである。日本側がこれを誤読し、「前二島」〈鬱陵島・独島〉をもって日本の西北部の限界としたのは大きな誤りである。隠州をもって日本の西北部の限界とするという隠州視聴合記の記事こそ正当な見解と見なければならない。（二四二～二四三頁）（乙）

一九七八年

【梶村秀樹】

日本側の文献上の竹島＝独島の初出は、ずっと遅く出雲藩士斎藤豊仙編の『隠州視聴合記』（一六六七年刊）で、「竹島」（鬱陵島）と別に「松島」という名で記載されている。（一八頁）（甲）

『隠州視聴合記』の表現は、韓国側の指摘のように、隠州を日本の境域の限界とのべたものと解すべきだろう。（二二頁）（乙）

一九八五年

【宋炳基】

…一六六七年（寛文七年、顕宗八年）に著述された「隠州視聴合記」に

雲州在北海中　故隠岐嶋…其府者　周吉郡南岸西郷豊崎也、…戌亥間　行二日一夜有松島、又一日程　有竹島〔原注〕、「俗言磯竹島、多竹魚海鹿」、二此島　無人之地　見高麗　如自雲州望隠岐　然則日本乾地　以此州為限矣

と見えるのがそれである。隠岐（隠州）の府治から二日一夜を行けば松島があり、さらに一日ほど行けば竹島がある。この二島は無人島であり、「高麗」を見ること、ちょうど出雲国（雲州）から隠岐を眺めるのと同じである。したがって日本の西北境（乾地）は「隠州」をもって限界とするというのである。地理的位置から見ると松島は今日の独島、竹島は鬱陵島を指すのであり、この二島は朝鮮に近いので、日本の領土は「隠州」すなわち隠岐に限られるということである。「隠州視聴合記」の著者斎藤豊仙は出雲国の官員で

あった。彼はまた藩主の命にしたがって公務で隠岐島を視察した。そして視察の過程で彼が直接見たり聞いたりしたものをそのまま記録したのが、この「隠州視聴合記」である。したがって、彼が「日本乾地 以此州為限矣」としているのは、当時の韓日間の国境を見極めるうえで、信憑性のある重要な史料となるものといえる。(『独島研究』二〇〇~二〇一頁)(乙)

独島(リャンコ島・竹島)に関する日本最古で古典的な文献は、一六六七年斎藤豊仙が日本沿海(隠岐)民から聞いた逸話・伝説をもとにして著述した。「隠州視聴合記」である。この文献に見える「竹島」と「松島」はまさに今日の鬱陵島と独島を指している。これは日本が一七世紀中葉から独島を松島と呼んでいたことを意味している。しかしこの文献は同時に、日本の版図を隠州に限らせることにより松島をその領域外へと外している。少なくとも松島が日本の版図ではないということは明白であった。(『独島研究』二六〇~二六一頁)(甲)

【崔爽祐】

日本側文献に鬱陵島とは別に今日の独島が認知される最初の記録は、おおむね一六六七年すなわち朝鮮王朝顕宗八年、日本出雲藩の藩士斎藤豊仙が編纂したという「隠州視聴合記」なる書であるようだ。(甲)一六六七年八月に命を受け、隠岐島を巡行し、その見聞録として書いたという「隠州視聴合記」の巻一国代記には、次のような内容がある。

隠州 在北海中 故云隠岐嶋…従是南方至雲州美穂関三十五里 辰巳至伯州赤碕浦四十里 未申至石州温泉津五十八里 自子至卯

無可往地 戌亥間行二日一夜有松島 又一日程有竹島(俗言磯竹島 多竹魚鹿) 此二島無人之地 見高麗如自雲州望隠岐 然則日本之乾地 以此州為限矣…

この記録にみえる竹島は今日の隠岐島から戌亥のあいだすなわち西北方へ船で二日一夜の距離にあったというが、船の規模や波頭あるいは風速などが一定しないから、ちょうど二日一夜の距離なのかははっきりとはしないが、のちにも今日の独島に比定される島嶼を日本側では松島と呼ぶ記録がある点などを勘案すると、いったん現在の独島を指すものとしても構わないようである。

この記録によれば独島(松島)と鬱陵島(竹島)がいずれも無人島だとするが、独島はもちろん無人島であったとしてよいが鬱陵島までも無人であったとできるかは疑問である。それはともかく、この記録によれば、この二島から高麗を見ることは日本から雲州すなわち出雲地方から西北の土地は「此州」すなわち隠州を見るのと同じであり、したがって日本の乾地すなわち西北すなわち隠州をもって限界となるという。言い換えれば「隠州視聴合記」で、今日の独島が松島という名前で認知されている事実は認められるものの、そのことは鬱陵島すなわちこの記録にいう竹島とともに日本領土の西北方限界の外にあると認識されていたことが分かる。「隠州視聴合記」では日本領土の西北限界が現在の隠岐島と認識されていたということである。(『独島研究』二八九~二九〇頁)(乙)

【白忠鉉】

さらに独島に関する最初の日本側記録である隠州視聴合記(一六

六七）にも隠州からいくらか行くと松島（独島）が現れ、さらに行くと竹島（鬱陵島）が現れるといい、"日本の国境は此州で限る"と記録されているが、これはまさに松島からは外国と見ていたと解釈しなければならず、日本側主張のように松島までを隠州に含んでいたと見ることはできない。（『独島研究』四二九～四三〇頁）（乙）

＊李漢基を引用する。

一九八七年

【堀和生】

日本の文献で、今日の竹島が初出するのは、出雲藩士斎藤豊仙の『隠州視聴合記』（一六六七年）であり、松島の名称で竹島＝鬱陵島と併記されている。（一〇一頁）（甲）

一九八九年

【慎鏞廈】

『隠州視聴合記』…日本で鬱陵島と独島に関する記録が最初に現れるのは、一六六七年斎藤豊仙が編纂した『隠州視聴合記』においてである。（甲）

ところで、この日本側史料は発掘者の意図とは異なり、鬱陵島と独島が高麗（韓国）の領土であり、日本の領土ではないことを明白に証明している。

「隠州在北海中　故云隠岐島…戌亥間　行二日一夜有松島　又一日程有竹島（俗言磯竹島多竹魚鹿　按神書所謂五十猛歟）此二島無人之地　見高麗如自雲州望隠州　故日本之乾地　以此州為限矣」【隠州は北海のなかにある。それで隠岐島という。…戌亥間に二日一夜行けば松島がある。さらに一日の距離のところに竹島がある。（俗言に磯竹島と呼ぶが、竹や魚やおっとせいが多い。神書にいういわゆる五十猛である）。この二島（松島と竹島）は無人島であり、高麗を見るのがちょうど雲州から隠岐を見るのと同じである。そういうわけで日本の西北（乾）境地はこの州（隠州）をもって限りとする。

すなわち日本で最初に鬱陵島と独島を記録したこの『隠州視聴合記』は、位置の上から見ると独島を松島、鬱陵島を竹島と呼びながら、この二島から高麗を見ることは、ちょうど日本の雲州（出雲国）から隠岐を見るのと同じであり、この二島松島と竹島は隠州に属しており、日本の西北境界地は隠州（隠岐島）をもって限界とすることを明らかにしている。この『隠州視聴合記』の編纂者斎藤豊仙は出雲（雲州）の官吏（藩士）として藩主の命を受け一六六七年（日本の寛文七年）夏に隠岐島を巡見し採録し『隠州視聴合記』をもって復命したのである。日本で最初に鬱陵島と独島を記録したこの文献は、鬱陵島と独島は高麗（韓国）の固有領土であって日本の領土ではないという事実をよく証明している。（四九～五〇頁）（乙）

一九九一年

【慎鏞廈】

斎藤は出雲（雲州）の官吏（藩士）として藩主の命を受け、一六六七年（日本、寛文七年）夏、隠岐島を巡見し、見聞を記録して『隠州視聴合記』を著した。本書は、日本では独島を"松島"と、鬱陵島を"竹島"と呼んだ事実を、航海距離（日数）を通じて間接

的に証明している。

隠岐は北海のなかにある。それで隠岐島という。…戌亥間に二日一夜行けば松島がある。さらに一日の距離のところに竹島)がある。〈俗言に磯竹島と呼ぶが、竹や魚やおっとせいが多い。神書にいういわゆる五十猛であろうか)。この二島(松島と竹島)は無人島であり、高麗を見るのがちょうど雲州から隠岐を見るのと同じである。そういうわけで日本の西北〔乾〕境地はこの州(隠州) をもって限りとする。

われわれがここでまた注目するのは、日本で最初に鬱陵島と独島を記録した文献だという《隠州視聴合記》は、〔甲〕日本で独島を松島、鬱陵島を竹島としていたこととともに、この二島から高麗を見ることはちょうど日本の雲州(出雲国)から隠岐を見るのと同じであり、この二島、松島と竹島は高麗に属することを教えてくれ、したがって日本の西北方の境界は隠州(隠岐島)をもって限界とすることを明白に証明しているという事実である。(慎鏞厦九六)五九～六〇頁)

そののち日本の出雲〔雲州〕の官吏〔藩士〕として藩主の命を受け、一六六七年(日本の寛文七年)夏、隠岐島を巡見し、その見聞を採録して復命した斎藤豊仙も、その文章《隠州視聴記》で—さきにも述べたように—日本の西北境界が隠州(隠岐島)をもって限りとすると書いており、松島(独島)と竹島〔鬱陵島〕の位置を正確に叙述しつつ、これらが高麗〔韓国〕の領土だと記録した。(慎鏞厦九六)一二五～一二六頁)(乙)

＊ここでは〔慎鏞厦九六〕第二部によるが、初出は『韓国社会史研究会論文集』二七、一九九一年。

一九九六年
【李薫】

独島の存在を最も早く記録しているものとして《隠州視聴合記》がある。〔甲〕出雲州の藩士斎藤豊仙が領主の命を受け、一六六七年に隠岐を巡視したち報告用に作成した本書には、"竹島(鬱陵島)と松島(独島)は無人島で、ここから高麗(朝鮮)を見るのはちょうど雲州から隠岐を見るのと同じである"としており、鬱陵島・独島が朝鮮の土地であることはもちろんのこと、日本の西北境界が隠岐であることを分明にしている。(一九～二〇頁)(乙)

【慎鏞厦ａｂ】

日本政府は、独島に関する日本側最初の文献として[1]一六六七年に編纂された《隠州視聴合記》を挙げている。〔甲〕本書は、出雲(雲州)[2]の官人〔藩士〕斎藤豊仙が藩州(大名)[3]の命を受け、一六六七年夏に隠岐島(玉岐島)[4]を巡視し、観察したり聞いたりしたことを採録して提出した報告書である[5]。ところでこの書にも独島と鬱陵島は高麗(朝鮮)に属し[6]、隠岐は日本に属し、隠岐が日本の西北方の限界だという趣旨を以下のように記録した。

隠岐は北海のなかにある。それで隠岐島という。…戌亥間に二日一夜行けば松島(当時、独島の日本側呼称—引用者)がある。さらに一日の距離のところに竹島(当時、鬱陵島の日本側呼称—引用者)[7]がある。…この二島(松島と竹島)は無人島であり、高麗を見るのがちょうど雲州から隠岐を見るのと同じである。そういうわけで日本の西北〔乾〕境地はこの州(隠州)をもって限

りとする。(*8)

日本最初の独島関連文献である《隠州視聴合記》は、官庁の報告
書であり、日本の西北国境を隠州をもって限りとする明白に規定し
ており(*9)、これは松島と竹島を高麗のものとして分類していると
言えまいか。とすれば、これは独島が韓国領土であることについての明白な証
明にほかならない。これは今日日本政府が日本の西北側
国境を鬱陵島と独島のあいだに設定していることが(*10)、どれほど荒
唐無稽なごり押しであり暴言であるかを、あらためてよく証明して
くれる。《新東亜》五九三～五九四頁、【慎鏞廈九六】二九～三〇
頁。

(乙)

*初出は、独島学会創立記念学術シンポジウム主題発表論文
(一九九六年四月)、韓国精神文化研究院独島問題学術会議主題発
表論文、《新東亜》一九九六年四月号の三論稿というが、ここで
は【慎鏞廈九六】第一部収録分をもとに、《新東亜》論稿との異
同を注記した。

(*1)　「文献」は、《新東亜》論稿では「記録文献」とする。
(*2)　「藩州」は、《新東亜》論稿では「領主」とする。
(*3)　「提出した報告書である」は、《新東亜》論稿では
　　　「隠州視聴合記」という題目をつけて報告書を提出し
　　　たのである」とする。
(*4)　「隠岐」は、《新東亜》論稿では「隠岐島」とする。
(*5)　「隠岐が日本の西北方の限界だという趣旨を以下のよ
　　　うに記録した」は、《新東亜》論稿では「日本の果て
　　　だと記録した」とする。
(*6)　「隠岐」は、《新東亜》論稿では「隠州」とする。

(*7)　「境地」は、《新東亜》論稿では「境界」とする。
(*8)　《新東亜》論稿は、このうしろに典拠名「隠州視聴合
　　　記」巻一、国代記」を記す。
(*9)　「日本の西北国境を隠岐をもって限りとする明白に規
　　　定しており」は、《新東亜》論稿では「日本の西北国
　　　境は隠州(現在の玉岐島)が果てであると明白に規定
　　　している」とする。
(*10)　「日本の西北側国境は、《新東亜》論稿では「日本の西北国
　　　境を鬱陵島と独島のあいだに設定し
　　　ていることが」は、《新東亜》論稿では「地理付図に
　　　日本の西北側国境を鬱陵島と独島のあいだに設定しよ
　　　うと試みていることは」とする。

【慎鏞廈C】

日本側調査によれば、日本の文献のなかで竹島〔鬱陵島〕ととも
に松島〔独島〕が最初に記録されているのは、一六六七年に編纂さ
れた《隠州視聴合記》である。〔甲〕本書は、編纂者斎藤豊仙が出
雲の官員(藩士)として藩主の命を受け、一六六七年(日本の寛文
七、朝鮮の顕宗八)夏に隠岐島を巡回しながら調査し、観察したり
聞いたりしたままを採録して報告書したものである。本書には次の
ように記録されている。

隠州は北海のなかにある。それで隠岐島という。…戌亥間に二
日一夜行けば松島(独島―引用者)があり、さらに一日の距離の
ところに竹島(鬱陵島―引用者)がある。(俗言に磯竹島という
が、竹や魚やオットセイが多い。神書にいういわゆる五十猛であ
るか)この二島(松島と竹島)は無人島であり、高麗を見るのが

ちょうど雲州から隠岐を見るのと同じである。そういうわけで日本の西北（乾）境地はこの州［隠州］をもって限りとする。

本書では日本の隠岐島から西北方へ船で二日一夜の距離に竹島があり、松島から一日距離に竹島があるとしており、位置と距離から判別すると松島と竹島を独島［于山島］を松島、鬱陵島を竹島と呼んでおり、この二島（松島と竹島）から高麗を見るのが、ちょうど日本の雲州（出雲国、現在の島根県）から隠岐島を見るのと同じであり、この二島松島［独島］と竹島［鬱陵島］は高麗に属し、したがって日本の西北境界は隠州をもって限界とすることが明らかである。

日本で最初に独島を記録したこの文献は、鬱陵島［竹島］と独島［松島］が高麗（韓国）領土を記録した島としていて、日本領土ではないという事実を明らかにしている。（乙）

【梶村秀樹】

日本側文献に竹島すなわち独島が初めて現れるのは出雲藩士斎藤豊仙編の『隠州視聴合記』（一六六七年刊行）で、韓国側に比べるとたいへん遅い。ここには「竹島」（鬱陵島）と区別された「松島」という名で記載されている。（六一七頁）（甲）

『隠州視聴合記』の表現は、韓国側の主張の如く隠州を日本の境界だと述べていると理解しなければならない。（六二〇頁）（乙）

【下條正男】

『隠州視聴合記』は、寛文七年（一六六七年）八月、藩命を受けた松江藩の斉藤矛緩が約二ヶ月を掛け、その預り領の隠岐島を巡察した際の調査報告書である。この『隠州視聴合記』は、竹島問題が発生して以来、日韓双方で竹島を自国領とする証左とされてきた。それは巻一の「国代記」に、松嶋（元竹島）と竹嶋（元鬱陵島）の二島が見え、その読み方によっては、竹島が朝鮮領とも解釈ができるからである。

そこで多少煩瑣となるが、理解を妨げない程度で一部を省略し、当該箇所を紹介してみたいと思う。

①隠州（隠岐島）は北海中にあり。（中略）

②是（隠岐島）より南、雲州美穂関に至ること三十五里。辰巳（南東）伯州赤碕浦に至ること四十里。未申（南西）石州温泉津に至ること五十八里。子（北）より卯（東）に至りては、往くべきの地なし。

③戌亥（北西）の間、行二日一夜にして竹嶋（現鬱陵島）あり、また一日の程にして竹島（現鬱陵島）あり。

④（註）俗に磯竹島という。竹魚海鹿多し。按ずるに、神書の所謂五十猛（イソタケ）歟。

⑤此の二嶋、無人の地。高麗（朝鮮）を見ること雲州より隠州を望むがごとし。

⑥然らばすなわち、日本の乾（北西）の地、此の州を以て限りとなす。

ここで斉藤矛緩が記述しているのは、北海の中にある竹島が、東西南北それぞれの方角にある日本の領土から、どれ程の位置にあるかである。当然これはそれぞれの地域にある日本の領土を中心に、放射状に結ばれていると考えてよく、隠岐島から北西の位置にある③の竹嶋（現鬱陵島）は、日本の再北西にある領土と認識されていたと解釈してよい。

ところが最近、『新東亜』九六年四月号に竹島問題を発表された

慎鏞廈氏は、右の「国代記」の文章から、②と④を抜き、①と③⑤を結んで、⑥の「此の州をもって限りとなす」の此の州を隠岐島のことと解釈し、『隠州視聴合記』も松嶋（現竹島）を朝鮮領としていたと結論を下していた。

しかしその解釈は、①と③と⑤を結んだ限りではそう読めないこともないが、資料は全体を見て正確に読まねばならぬのである。②を読まずにこの史料を解釈すると、隠岐島が日本の各地からどの方角で、どれほどの距離にあるかを示した斉藤矛緩の意図を抹殺し、文意を変えてしまうからである。

そして③の「戊亥（北西）」と、⑥の「日本の乾（北西）の地」から直接「此の州を以て限りとなす」に繋ぎ、此の州を隠州（隠岐島）とすると、松嶋（竹島）は朝鮮領であるかのような錯覚を与えるが、それは無理な解釈である。まず⑤の「高麗を見ること雲州の隠州を望むがごとし」は、高麗（朝鮮）を見ている位置は当然日本領という文章としているわけで、竹島、欝陵島、隠岐島の中で雲州（島根）から隠岐島を見るように朝鮮が見えるのは、欝陵島だけしかないからである。従って慎鏞廈氏が引用した文章だけから見ても、此の州を以て限りとするのは、欝陵島ということになる。

それを慎氏は何ら疑うことなく、「此の州」を「隠州」のこととされているが、「州」には「島」の意味があり、欝陵島を隠州とするように「此の州」を欝陵島のこととしても問題はないのである。現に李瀷も「星湖僿説類選」の中で、安龍福の功で欝陵島が朝鮮に復したことを「一州の土を復す」と記しているからだ。

史料はやはり一部を読んで解釈するのではなく、全体を見て読むべきではなかろうか。

慎氏はまた隠岐島を日本の北西の限りとされたが、それでは隠岐島を北西の限りとする基準点はどこに置くのであろうか。江戸（東京）をその中心に据えれば隠岐島は西にあたる。これは「国代記」の②を省略せずに史料を解釈してみると、その中心点が隠岐島にあることは明白である。慎氏が解釈されているように、中心点に据えた隠岐島を日本の北西の限りとするのでは、斉藤矛緩が隠岐島を基点とした意味がなくなってしまう。

これはもう少し慎重に史料を読むべきではなかろうか。それは④の註も抹殺すべき部分ではないということだ。この註には欝陵島が俗に磯竹島（イソタケシマ）と呼ばれている理由を、『日本書紀』の「神代巻」に登場する「五十猛神」に求め、斉藤矛緩自身が考証している部分だからだ。『隠州視聴合記』の著者が磯竹島を朝鮮領と認識していれば、そういった按語を書くはずもない。この註なども斉藤矛緩が磯竹島（欝陵島）を自国領と認識していた証左の一つである。

さらに当時、斉藤矛緩が欝陵島を以て日本の北西限とし、欝陵島を日本領と認識していたことは、『隠州視聴合記』の「知夫郡焼火山縁起」の文中からも指摘することができる。

同縁起には「時に元和四年春三月、又伯耆国の大賈村河氏、官より朱印を賜り大船を磯竹島に到す。颶風に遇して高句麗に落つ」と記されている。この縁起では朝鮮とあるべきところ高句麗と表記しているが、これは縁起であるため古色蒼然とさせるための作文である。元和四年は一六一八年で新しく、文中の村河氏は、後年、安龍福を拉致した大谷氏と並んで幕府から欝陵島での漁採を許されていた。この「知夫郡焼火山縁起」を含む『隠州視聴合記』が成立する

のは、一六六七年一〇月。日本と朝鮮の間ではまだ鬱陵島問題が発生しておらず、李睟光の『芝峰類説』が「倭奴磯竹島を占拠す」とした時代で、日本側が鬱陵島を自国領と認識し、実質的にも漁場としていたことは、斉藤矛綏も知っていたはずである。

それは朝鮮との間に鬱陵島問題が起きた時、朝鮮側が三百年間政策的に無人島化していたからである。実際的には鬱陵島が放置された状態にあったからである。日本側としてはすでに光海君七年（一六一四年）、朝鮮側に鬱陵島探索の可否を告げていたが、朝鮮側からは正式な回答がなく、以来日本側は実質的に漁撈の場としていたのである。事実この経緯は、『粛宗実録』二〇年（一六九四年）八月己酉条で、南九萬が粛宗に「倭の此島（鬱陵島）で漁採すること、また久し」と、鬱陵島帰属問題の経緯を奏上した際にも確認されている。

斉藤矛綏が、『隠州視聴合記』を著述するのは、その二七年前のことである。この時、斉藤矛綏は鬱陵島を朝鮮領と見做すであろうか。それは当時の時代状況から判断しても有り得ないことである。

従って斉藤矛綏は『隠州視聴合記』で、「然らば則ち日本の乾（北西）の地、此の州を以て限りとなす」とする此の州は、隠州ではなく鬱陵島でなければならないのである。でなければ安龍福と李於屯が領海侵犯の証拠に拉致され、三年にもわたって鬱陵島の領有権問題が日韓で争われることもなかったはずである。

『隠州視聴合記』の此の州は、鬱陵島であったのである。（六八～七一頁）（乙）

【クック・チャンコン】

ところで先の、「隠州視聴合記」の最後の一節「というわけで日本の西北地は此州をもって境界として限る」の「此州」は通常は隠州を指すことが明らかであるのに、下條氏は「州」が島だという意味もあるから」という変わった前提のもと、二つの無人島（鬱陵島・独島）だと解釈しているのは、それこそあきれたごり押しである。

「州」（行政単位の州）が島の意であることもあるが、この場合「洲」（島の洲）の字を使って洲島・洲嶋など慣用句として用い、州は州郡県・州国のように用いる。二つの無人島を州とか、松島（独島）を松州などとすることは全くない。

さらに「というわけで日本の西北地は此州をもって境界として限る」にいう「此州」は、まさにこの報告書の主題（隠州視聴合記）であるとともに、冒頭にある「隠州は…」とおしまいあたりの此州の直前に現れる州名を受けて、隠州が日本国の境界の限りであるというのである。（一三五頁）（乙）

【金炳烈】

「隠州視聴合記」は斎藤豊仙が隠岐島地方を巡視して一六六七年になったの風土記である。一九五〇年代に韓日間で独島領有権論争がおこったとき、日本側が領有権主張の資料として提示したものの、かえって韓国の領有権を立証する羽目に陥ることとなった資料である。

そののち日本側ではこの件につきふたたび取り上げることがないままだが、問題となっている原文は

隠州在北海中故云隠岐嶋…従是南方至雲州美穂関三十五里　辰巳

至伯州赤碕浦四十里　未申至石州温泉津五十八里　自子至卯無可往地　戌亥間行二日一夜有松島　又一日程有竹島（俗言磯竹島　多竹魚海鹿）　此二島無人之地　見高麗如自雲州望隠州　然則日本之乾地　以此島為限矣、である。

　下條氏は〝現代コリア〟五月号で、①隠州を中心として、方向および距離を表示したため、独島と鬱陵島が隠州に含まれ、②〝見高麗如自雲州望隠州〟という表記から、眺めている位置は当然日本領土だと認識しており、③此州の州は隠州ではなく、④鬱陵島であるとして、〝州＝島〟の様な意味だから此州は鬱陵島であり、鬱陵島の俗称は〝日本書紀〟の様に現れる〝五十猛神〟にもとづく磯竹島だと主張している。

　まず①をみよう。隠州を中心にして方向および距離を表示すれば隠州の領域に含まれることになるのか？とすれば隠州を中心に何里式に表記された伯州赤碕浦、石州温泉津がすべて隠州に含まれるということなのか？下條氏の論理でゆけば、韓国側記録に、釜山から対馬島が何里、釜山から長崎が何里式に表記されているから、対馬島・長崎も韓国領と認めなくてはなるまい。

　②の場合、眺めている位置だから日本領だという主張も理屈に合わない。それは当時鬱陵島近海で漁労作業をしていた漁夫たちから伝聞した内容を記録してそうなっただけである。対馬島から釜山が見えると記録されているから釜山が日本領であり、釜山から対馬島が見えると記録されているから韓国領だということになるのか？

　③で下條氏が主張するように州が島の意味である場合には、見る方向が重要だともいえるが、この場合は全くそうではない。しかしこうした意味で用いる場合には、群島だとか行政体制をもつ集落がある場合にのみ該当する。隠岐島が隠州と分離されているのもこれと同じ理由からである。下條氏が例にあげた〝星湖僿説類選〟にある安龍福の功労で取り戻したとする一州は、鬱陵島とその属島を含む意味であることは明らかである。

　④磯竹島という名のゆえに鬱陵島が日本領だという主張も正しくない。元来、鬱陵島の聖人峰を韓国人たちは〝コムスリ（熊鷲）〟と呼んできたが、それを漢字で音訳表記して〝弓嵩〟とした。これは〝おそろしい＝神聖〟な峰という意味である。だからいまも聖人峰と呼んでいるのである。

　こうした弓嵩という表記は日本にも伝えられ、一七八九年浪華書林で製作された〝朝鮮世表全図〟と一八〇六年に林が製作した〝朝鮮八道地図〟等を見ると、欝陵島内に山を描き、そこに弓嵩と記し、かなでイソタケと併記していることが分かる。

　すなわち弓嵩の意を意訳し磯竹島としたのであって、のちにこれを再び漢字で音訳するのではない。万一五十猛神に由来したのであれば、その周辺の他の島々にも神の名が付けられていなければならないのではないか。

　したがって、〝隠州視聴合記〟の州は隠州とみるのが、文章上も意味上も妥当だということである。（一九四～一九六頁）〔乙〕

一九九九年
〔河錬洙〕

　この松島（今日の竹島）が日本の歴史的文献において初めてみられるのは、一六六七年編纂された『隠州視聴合記』巻一国代記にお

いてであると言われている。すなわち、その記録には「隠州在二北
海中一。故云二隠岐嶋一、…戌亥間行二日一夜有二松島一、又一日程有二
竹島一(俗言磯竹島多竹魚海鹿按神書所謂五十猛歟)此二島無レ人
之地、見二高麗一如レ自二雲州一望二隠州一。然則日本之乾地以二此州一為レ
限矣」と、今日の竹島に対する認知が明記されている。(二四四頁)
(甲)

　＊川上健三を引用する。

二〇〇〇年
【内藤正中】

一六六七年(寛文七)に、松江藩士の斎藤豊仙が著した『隠州
視聴合紀』では、朝鮮との国境について次のように記している。

「隠州在北海中　故云二隠岐嶋一…戌亥間　行二日一夜有二松島一　又一
日程有竹島〈割注：俗言磯竹島　多竹魚海鹿〉　此二島無二人之地
見高麗　如自雲州望隠岐　然則日本為レ限」

この記述は、幕府の特別許可を得て竹島渡海事業を営んでいた伯
耆国米子町人の船が、竹島往復の途中で入手した松島(元竹島)に
ついての知見が隠岐の国内に伝えられ、斉藤の知るところとなって
記されたものである。それが竹島(鬱陵島)とともに松島について
も記していることから注目されているところであり、さらには現在
の竹島(独島)領有権にも関わる問題として、特に「日本乾地以此
州為レ限」の文言が意味するところをめぐって、日韓両国の学者の
見解は対立したままで現在に至っている。対立している論点は、日
本の西北境を竹島(鬱陵島)とする日本
側に対して、韓国側では隠州(隠岐国)と見ているところである。

しかし一六九六年(元禄九)の竹島一件が結着する以前の時期で
ある一六六七年にまとめられた文献である以上、幕府の特別許可を
得て竹島渡海事業が行われている時期であるから、竹島(鬱陵島)
を日本の乾地(西北境)と思って記述したことは当然と見なければ
ならない。なお、一八三三年(文政六)の大西教保による『隠岐古
記集』では、「此島より朝鮮を望免は隠州より雲州を見るより猶遠
して、今は朝鮮人来て住すと言ふ」と記し、「此島」が竹島(鬱陵
島)であることを明らかにしている。本書は前述『隠州視聴合紀』
を底本にして、さらに増補したものといわれている「日本視
聴合紀』における「日本乾地」は竹島(鬱陵島)となる。(一二一
～一二三頁)(乙)

二〇〇一年
【慎鏞廈】

日本政府が独島に関する日本側最初の文献として挙げるのは、一
六六七年に編纂されたこの『隠州視聴合記』である。(甲)ところ
で本書にも独島と鬱陵島は高麗(朝鮮)に属し、隠岐は日本に属す
のであって、隠岐が日本の西北方の限界だという趣旨を以下のよう
に記録した。

隠岐は北海のなかにある。それで隠岐島という。…戌亥間に二
日一夜行けば松島(当時、独島の日本側呼称…引用者)がある。
さらに一日の距離のところに竹島(当時、鬱陵島の日本側呼称…
引用者)がある。…この二島(松島と竹島)は無人島であり、高
麗を見るのがちょうど雲州から隠岐を見るのと同じである。そう
いうわけで日本の西北(乾)境地はこの州(隠州)をもって限り

とする。

日本最初の独島関連文献である『隠州視聴合記』は、官庁の報告書であり、日本の西北国境を隠岐をもって限りとする明白に規定しており、松島と竹島を高麗のものとして分類しているのである。これは独島が韓国領土であることについての明白な証明にほかならない。とすれば、これは今日日本政府が〝松島渡海免許〟をもって独島の固有領土論を証明しながら、日本の西北側国境を鬱陵島と独島のあいだに設定しようとすることが、どれほど荒唐無稽なごり押しであり暴言であるかを、あらためてよく証明してくれる。(一一~一二頁)(乙)

＊[慎鏞廈二〇〇三、一二六~一二七頁]にもほぼ同文あり。

二〇〇四年
【下條正男】

…日本政府が竹島の歴史的権原を示す文献としている出雲藩の斎藤豊仙が編述した『隠州視聴合記』(一六六七年序)に対しても、韓国側は別の解釈を示した。『隠州視聴合記』の「国代記」には「日本の乾(北西)の地、此を以て限りと為す」と記されていることから、日本政府はこの「国代記」にある「此州」を鬱陵島のことと解釈し、それより東にある竹島は、日本領であると解釈した。ところが、『韓国の領土』(一九六九年刊)の著者である李漢基氏は、「〈隠州視聴合記〉を」精読すると、隠州(隠岐島)を日本の乾(西北限界)としていることは分明である。日本側は鬱陵島を日本の乾(北西)と独島が西北限界と誤読している」と主張したのである。

さらに慎鏞廈氏も『独島の民族領土史研究』(一九九六年刊)で、「此州」を隠岐島と解釈し、「日本側の資料は、発掘者の意図とは異なり、鬱陵島と独島が高麗の領土であり、日本の領土でないことを明白に示している」と決めつけたのである。

しかし慎鏞廈氏は、後に述べるように、『隠州視聴合記』から自説に都合のよい箇所だけを抜き出して解釈し、「国代記」の文章全体を読んでいなかったのである。両氏は、「此州」が日本の北西限である理由を説明した最も重要な箇所を無視し、斎藤豊仙は鬱陵島を日本領としていた、とする日本側の解釈を、「誤読」と断言しているのである。

では、実際の『隠州視聴合記』の「国代記」にはどのように記述されていたのだろうか。文章を損なわない程度に簡略にして引用すると、次の通りである。(カッコ内は筆者注)。

(一) 隠州(隠岐島)は北海の中にあり。【中略】

(二) 是(隠岐島)より南、雲州(出雲)美穂(保)関に至ること三十五里。

(三) 辰巳(南東)、伯州(伯耆)赤碕浦に至ること四十里。

(四) 未申(南西)、石州(石見)温泉津に至ること五十八里。

(五) 子(北)より卯(東)に至りては、往くべきの地なし。

(六) 戌亥(北西)の間、行くこと二日一夜にして松嶋(現在の竹島)あり。また一日の程にして竹嶋(現在の鬱陵島)あり。【中略】此二嶋、無人の地。高麗を見ること雲州より隠州を望むが如し。

(七) 然らば則ち、日本の乾(北西)の地、此の州を以て限りと

為す。

この「国代記」を素直に読めば、斎藤豊仙の意図は明らかである。斎藤豊仙は（二）以下で、隠岐島を基準として、隠岐島からの方位と距離を記し、隠岐島とその周辺の地域との地理的関係を示していたのである（前ページの図（＊）参照）。そして（六）では、隠岐島から見て、北西の間にある日本の領土として松嶋（現在の竹島）と竹嶋（現在の鬱陵島）を挙げ、そこからは、雲州（出雲）から隠州（隠岐島）が見えるように高麗（朝鮮）が見える、とその地理的特性を示したのである。

したがって、この論法からすれば、（七）に記された「此州」がどこの島を指しているのかは明白である。隠岐島を基点に乾（北西）の方角にあって、最も朝鮮半島に近い「州（島）」といえば、竹嶋（鬱陵島）の他にはない。「此州」は、李漢基氏や慎鏞廈氏が主張するような隠岐島ではありえないのである。

ところが、李漢基氏や慎鏞廈氏ら韓国側の研究者は、この「国代記」の記述のうち（一）と（七）だけを引用して、日本の『隠州視聴合記』も隠岐島を日本の北西限としていた、と反論しているのである。

明らかにそれは牽強付会の説である。それでは（七）の前に、接続詞の「然らば」を入れた意味がなくなってしまう。ここでの「然らば」の役割は、雲州（出雲）より隠州（隠岐島）を望むがごとく、竹嶋（鬱陵島）から高麗（朝鮮）が望めることにあるからである。そして、日本領から高麗（朝鮮）が望めるのは、竹嶋「国代記」の中では鬱陵島だけである。

そもそも『隠州視聴合記』が書かれた当時の出雲藩には、竹嶋

（鬱陵島）を日本領として認識するだけの事情があった。隠岐島は一六三八（寛永十五）年以来一時期を除いて出雲藩の預かり領だったため、隠岐島の西郷には、出雲藩から派遣された郡代が詰めていた。したがって、一六九六（元禄九）年に江戸幕府が鬱陵島への渡航を禁ずるまで、鳥取藩から「往来手形」の発給を受けた米子の大谷、村川両家は、隠岐島の西郷に渡った出雲藩の番所に立ち寄っていたのである。こうした歴史があったため、鬱陵島に渡る際には、鬱陵島の西郷が鬱陵島に出漁していた事実を知っていたのである。

実際『隠州視聴合記』中の別の記事「知夫郡焼火山縁起」にも、「伯耆の国の大賈村河氏、官より朱印を賜り大船を磯竹島（鬱陵島のこと）に致す」と記されており、「南方村」条では、「磯（礒）竹嶋に渡る者是に於て泊して晴を量り風を占う」として鬱陵島への渡海に言及している。斎藤豊仙が鬱陵島を日本領として『隠州視聴合記』に書くのは当然のことなのである。（一六七～一七一頁）（乙）

注‥（甲）（乙）の記号は本文中の説明に一致する。

（いけうち・さとし　名古屋大学教授）

（＊）図は省略した。

第四章

隠岐の安龍福

『北東アジア文化研究』第 22 号、2005年 10月、1 - 15頁

內藤正中

島根大學 名譽教授,
前鳥取女子大學短期大學北東アジア總合文化研究所長兼客員教授

隠岐の安龍福

内 藤 正 中

（元鳥取短期大学北東アジア文化総合研究所所長・島根大学名誉教授）

An Ron Buk in Oki Island

NAITO Seichu

キーワード：領土紛争（territory dispute）、竹島＝独島（Takeshima
Island）、日朝関係史（history of Japan-Korea rela-
tions）

1 は じ め に

　日韓両国間で対立している竹島（独島）の領有権問題のなかで、必ず登場し
てくるのが安龍福である。朝鮮国慶尚道東萊の安龍福は、17世紀末に日本伯耆
国に来て、鳥取藩主から鬱陵島と子山島（独島）は朝鮮の領土であることを認
めた書契をもらったということで、独島の領有権を日本で主張した人物として、
韓国の中学高校の国史教科書で特筆されているのである。

　安龍福が日本で独島の領有権を主張したということは、『朝鮮王朝実録』な
どに記してある。ただしそれらの記録は、伯耆国から帰国した後に捕えられ取
り調べを受けた備辺司での供述がもとになっている。その供述の信憑性につい
て客観的に立証できる史料はなく、備辺司で同行者たちも同じようなことを述
べたと記すにとどまっているところに、安龍福の供述がもつ問題性があるとい
うべきであろう。何よりも、日本で起こった事件であるだけに、日本側とりわ
けて当事者である鳥取藩の記録とつき合せてみる必要がある。幸いなことには、
鳥取藩には池田家文書をはじめ、『因府年表』や『竹島考』などの関係史料が

2

あり、伯耆—因幡両国での安龍福の足跡や鳥取藩としての対応について知ることができるのである。このため私は、かつて『竹島（鬱陵島）をめぐる日朝関係史』（2000年、多賀出版）のなかで、因伯両国における安龍福について取り上げ解明したことがある。

　この安龍福について、1696（元禄9）年5月に隠岐国に着岸した時の取調記録が、島根県隠岐郡海士町の村上家で2005年5月に発見された。「元禄九丙午年朝鮮舟着岸一巻之覚書」である。

　海士町の村上家は、隠岐島前の公文役であり、松江藩預かりとなる1721（享保7）年から実施される大庄屋制では、島前二郡を代表する大庄屋となる。隠岐国は、1638（寛永15）年から1687（貞享4）年までは松江藩の預ケ地であったが、1688年から1720（享保5）年までの間は、幕府天領として石見国銀山料大森代官の管轄になっていた。したがって、代官所から派遣されていた隠岐の在番役人は人数も少なかったので、大庄屋は日常的に行政実務にたずさわっていた関係で、朝鮮船来着にさいしての取り調べにおいても立ち会って記録を残したものと思われる。

　1696（元禄9）年5月18日に、隠岐国島後の西村海岸に着岸した朝鮮船には、安龍福ら11人が乗っていた。取り調べたところ、安龍福は「朝鮮八道之図」を示し、日本で竹島、松島と呼んでいる島は朝鮮国江原道に属することを明らかにする。併せて自分たちは鳥取の伯耆守に訴願するために当地に立ち寄ったもので、順風を待って伯州に渡海するつもりであるとも語っている。

　安龍福らは6月4日に伯耆国赤崎に行く。隠岐国では5月23日付で、大森の石州御役所に「覚書」に書き留めたものを報告書として提出する。したがって、5月22日から6月4日までの間の隠岐滞在の状況については明らかにすることはできない。鳥取藩内に滞在中のことについては、鳥取藩の諸記録によって詳細を知ることができるが、城下入りをした6月21日を最後にして、8月6日に帰国してゆく50日間の記録は外聞をはばかってのためか、簡潔にまとめるかたちをとっている。

　そのために、『朝鮮王朝実録』などで安龍福が供述したことになっている、鳥取藩主に会って竹島、松島が朝鮮領の鬱陵島と子山島であることなどについ

て、ほんとうに主張したかどうかを確認することのできる鳥取藩側の史料はない。しかしながら、隠岐で代官役人が取り調べた「朝鮮舟着岸一巻之覚書」で明らかなように、竹島、松島が朝鮮領であることを主張するための準備をして、伯耆州をめざしてやってきた事実は確認できるのである。また、伯耆に着岸した時に、船首に「朝鬱両島監税将臣安同知騎」と墨書した旗をかかげていたことなども、隠岐で見られた領有権を主張するための準備の一環として理解できることになる。これらのことから、安龍福が備辺司で行った供述のすべてを自作自演の作り話として全否定する見解に対しては、見直してゆく必要があるのではないかと思っている。

　なお松島（現竹島、独島）は、朝鮮王朝の時代には「于山島」と呼ばれているが、安龍福は備辺司での供述のなかでも、そして隠岐でも「子山島」といっているので、本稿では「子山島」と記すことにする。

2　隠岐着岸の朝鮮船

　朝鮮船が隠岐島後の西村に着岸したのは、1696（元禄9）年5月18日であった。しかしそこは荒磯であったことから中村に行き、19日の夜に大久村のかよい浦に入り、20日になって西郷から駆けつけてきた在番役人による取り調べが行われた。22日に調べが終り、石州御役所に送る調書を作成するとともに、西郷に船を廻送しようとしたが、風雨が強かったため、そのまま大久村にいた。

　朝鮮船は、長さ3丈（9m）、幅1丈2尺（3.6m）、深さ4尺2寸（1.3m）の80石積みの船で、帆檣2、帆2、梶1、櫓5、木碇2を持っていた。船首には木綿の幟が2枚あったほか、楮が4房、敷物のござ、犬の皮があった。

　これら諸品については、別に「朝鮮舟在之道具之覚」として書き留められている。そこでは白米（叺に3合程残り申候）、和布3表、塩1表、干鮑1、薪1〆（長6尺8寸、但1尺廻り）、竹6本（長3尺5寸、同3尺）、刀1腰（此刀武具ニハ難用、鈍相成ニテノミ）、脇指1腰（脇指ニ候へ共、料理ナトイタシ候ニ付、包丁同然）、鑓4筋（何も鮑笠物之由、長物は4尺斗）、長刀1、半弓1、矢1箱、帆柱2本（内1本は8尋、1本は6尋、内1本は竹の由）、梶1羽（1丈4尺5寸）、みな王綱（わら、かづら）、とま10枚斗（内2枚長5

尺、横1丈2尺、残ハ日本ノとまヨリ少し大キ）、犬皮3枚、敷ござ3枚（帆
ござノ類ニテ候）であり、「右之通見分仕候処紛無御座候」とある。

　乗船していたのは11人であった。名前を書き出したのは、安龍福、李神元、
金可果、雷憲、衍習の5人で、年令を記したのは、安龍福、雷憲、衍習の3人
だけで、他の俗3人、僧3人は名前も年令も明らかにしなかった。

　安龍福は午歳の43才、冠のような黒い笠をかぶり、水精の緒、アサキ木綿の
上着、腰に通政大夫、申午生、住東莱、印彫入と記した札をつけていた。扇に
は小箱に入った印判、そして耳かき楊子の入った小箱をつけていた。

　金可果も冠のような黒い笠をかぶり、木綿の細白き上着をつけていたが、扇
は持っていない。年齢は不明。

　雷憲は興旺寺の住持で、年は55才。冠のような黒い笠、木綿の細美なる上着
をつけ、扇子を持っていた。金鳥山朱印の康煕8年閏3月20日と記した書付、
長さ1尺、幅4寸、高さ4寸の箱を持ち、その中には鈴の金具、竹で作った算
木、硯、筆墨があった。また珠数は日本の禅宗が使っているのと同じで、珠の
数は10ばかりであった。

　衍習は雷憲の弟子の僧、33才で、衣装は雷憲と同様である。

　他の僧3人は、竹島を見物するために同行したと述べている。

　以上が、乗船していた11人に対する調査の結果で、名前、年齢、衣服、持物
などが調べられている。なお名前については、雷憲以外の10人全員が、調査の

隠　　岐	伯　　者	帰　国　後
安龍福　43才	安同知（朝鬱両島監税將）	安龍福（東莱人）
李神元	李裸將（進士軍官）	李仁成（平山浦人）
金可果	金裸將（進士軍官）	金成吉（楽安人）
金耳官	金沙工（帯率）	
柳上工	劉格率（帯率）	劉日夫（興海人）
ユウカイ	劉漢夫（帯率）	劉奉石（寧海人）
雷　憲　55才	雷　憲（金鳥僧將釋氏）	雷　憲（順天僧）
衍　習　33才	習化主（釋氏帯率僧）	金順立（責延安人）
靈　律	律化主（釋氏帯率僧）	靈律丹（勝淡連習）
勝　淡	淡法主（釋氏帯率僧）	
丹　責	責　主（釋氏帯率僧）	
「朝鮮舟着岸一巻之覚書」	「竹島考」	「朝鮮王朝実録」

都度異なっていることが次の表からわかる。「伯耆」というのは、伯耆国に上陸して鳥取藩が調べたもので、『竹島考』による。「帰国後」とは『朝鮮王朝実録』で備辺司が調べた時のものである。

　着岸朝鮮人の取り調べは、11人のうち安龍福、雷憲、金可果の3人が代表して、在番役人に答えるかたちで行われた。そのさい安龍福が「通詞ニテ事ヲ問申候得バ、答申候」とあるように、安龍福が通訳になって日本語での質疑と応答が行われた。安龍福の日本語は、釜山の倭館に出入りして覚えたといわれているが、元禄6（1693）年に竹島から米子に連行された時も、「和語通詞」ということであった。ただし、隠岐のあと伯耆国へ行き、青谷の専念寺で鳥取藩の儒者と対談して以降は、城下鳥取に入っても日本語はわからないということで通している。

3　元禄6年の安龍福

　隠岐での在番役人の取り調べのなかで、安龍福は「四年己前酉夏竹島ニ而伯州之舟ニ被連まいり候」と、4年前の夏に伯耆の船によって竹島から連れてゆかれたと述べている。その時は、「とりべ」という者も一緒であったが、今回は竹島に残してきたと付け加えている。

　1696（元禄9）から4年前は1692年であるが、酉年は1693年である。その年3月に、アンビンシャ（安龍福）とトラヘ（朴於屯）の両人が、竹島から米子に連行されたのである。その時の日本側の記録は次の通りである。

　前年の1692（元禄5）年に竹島に渡海した村川船は、初めて朝鮮人に出会った。ただ朝鮮人は53人もいるのに日本側は21人であったから、朝鮮人が来ていたとする証拠の品だけを持って早々に引き揚げた。その時、朝鮮人のなかに日本語のわかる者がいたので、「此島之義公方様より拝領仕り、毎年渡海いたし候島にて候ところに、何とて参り候や」と、きびしく尋問したことを船頭の「口上之覚」は記している。

　そして1693年3月の大谷船の渡海である。この年も朝鮮人が先に来ており、そのなかに前年に出会った通詞の者がいたので、船に乗せて帰った。それは、昨年竹島に来てはいけないと強く叱りつけたにもかかわらず、今年も来ている

のは迷惑至極というべきで、きつく申し聞かせ断ってほしいと考えて米子に連
行してきたという。

　朝鮮人2人を連れて3月18日に竹島を出発、20日に隠岐の福浦に着き、そこ
で在番役人の取り調べを受けた。そして23日に福浦を出発するにあたり、2人
の朝鮮人に酒1樽が贈られたと船頭は述べている。その何故かはわからない。

　途中島前を経て27日に大谷船は米子に帰着、灘町の大谷九右衛門宅に収容さ
れる。鳥取藩は作廻人と警固の足軽2名を付けた。取り調べは、鳥取から家老
の荒尾大和とその伯父になる荒尾修理が派遣されて当り、1か月後の4月28日
になって「唐人の口書、並に所持候書三通」が鳥取の藩庁に送られ、30日には
そのまま江戸の藩邸に廻送されている。

　取り調べを終り、江戸からの指示を待っている間、鳥取藩の『控帳』5月11
日の條には、「アンビンシュン（和語通詞なり）気晴に出可申、色々わやく申
候由、修理迄申來候得共、外に出候事無用と差図申事、且又酒給申度由候得共、
是又畫夜に三升より上は無用の由、申達候事」とある。5月11日というと、3
月27日に米子に連行されて以来、50日近くにもなる。取り調べが終り、安龍福
の「口書」も提出されたことから、気晴らしのために外出したいと申し出たほ
か、いろいろ苦情を述べたようである。外出は許可されなかったが、1日3升
までは酒は飲んでもよいということになった。

　ここで和語通詞がアンビンシュンという名前であることが判明している。
1828（文政11）年に鳥取藩士の岡嶋正義がまとめた『竹島考』では、安龍福の
名前は竹島で出会った時に尋ねたことになっており、「吾在所ハ朝鮮国慶尚道
東萊県ノ者ニテ、アンビンシャ、年齢四十二オナリ、是ナル者ハ蔚山ノ人ニテ、
トラヘト云ヘリ、年齢ハ三十四オナリ」と答えたとしている。

　幕府の指示が出たのは5月26日であった。それは朝鮮人を陸路で長崎に送る
ようにというもので、『竹島考』には、「関東ノ御沙汰ヲ歴テ、政老中ヨリ朝鮮
人へハ、以来竹島へ渡海致サザル様ニ急度申含メ、肥前国長崎マデ送還スベキ
旨御裁定ナリ」と記している。

　『控帳』によれば、長崎送りに先だって朝鮮人を鳥取に連れてくるようにと
藩庁が命じている。このため、3名の組士を護衛に、医師もつけて米子から鳥

取に送った。鳥取の城下入りは6月1日で、まず家老の荒尾大和邸に入り、翌日から1週間は城下の会所に収容された。荒尾邸から会所に移した夜には、重臣4名が集ってわざわざ朝鮮人両名に会っている。物珍しさからどうかはわからない。なお、『竹島考』によれば、「アンピンシャハ猛性狂暴ナル者ノ由」とあり、『因府年表』では、「異客の内に暴悪の者これ有る由」と記し、そのためもあってか城下入りにあたっては、「女童出で候事無用」と、鳥取藩が触書を出している。

　長崎送りは、海上は心配であるとして陸上の道をとること、そして「萬々共御用意、夫々役人江申渡候事」と、鳥取藩として十分な配慮をして送り出した様子がうかがえる。道中は家臣2名が使者に任命され、医師、御徒方5名、軽卒御小人若干、脚力、それに料理人まで随行させている。6月7日に鳥取を出発同月30日に長崎到着、7月1日に長崎奉行所に2人の朝鮮人を引渡した。長崎では対馬藩留守居役に預けられて取り調べられ、8月14日に対馬藩から来た者に渡されて9月3日に対馬に着き、9月末に対馬藩の使者に連れられて帰国する。

　対馬藩の『朝鮮通交大紀』には、「元禄六癸酉年　此年　鈎命して朝鮮人四十余名、我因幡州竹島に来り漁せしによりて、其捕へたりし二名を彼国に送致せしむ。九月、公　多田与左衛門をして書を持らし、是を送られしの事」と見える。「我因幡州竹島」と記してあるのが注目される。

　これに対して韓国側の史料としては、『朝鮮王朝実録』その他がある。ここでは慎鏞廈の『史的解明独島（竹島）』（インター出版）のなかの記述についてみることにする。

　「数的に優勢であった日本人漁民たちが、朝鮮の蔚山のボス格である安龍福、朴
於屯らにゆっくり話し合おうと、うまく持ちかけて隠岐島に連行した。
　安龍福は隠岐島主に鬱陵島は朝鮮の領土であることを訴えた。そして朝鮮人が
自分の国の地に入っただけなのに何故に拉致したのかと抗議した。隠岐島主は上
司である伯耆藩の藩主に安龍福を引き渡した。そこでも安龍福は堂々と朝鮮領土
であることを主張した。そして日本は、日本人漁民が国境を越えて出漁するのを

取締まるべきだと要求した。

　当時の伯耆藩の藩主は、鬱陵島が朝鮮の領土であることを知っていたので、安龍福を江戸幕府に引き渡した。

　江戸幕府は安龍福を審問した結果、彼の主張に一貫性があり、事実を述べていることを認め、鬱陵島は日本の領土ではないという外交文書を伯耆藩の藩主に書かせ、安龍福らを江戸から長崎、対馬を経て朝鮮に送り返そうとした。

　しかし安龍福が長崎に着くと、対馬藩主は彼らを再び捕縛し、対馬へ連行し、そこで鬱陵島は日本領土でないと書いてある外交文書を奪い、彼を日本領土である鬱陵島を侵犯した罪人あつかいにし、朝鮮の東萊府で朝鮮側に不法な要求をつきつけて彼を釈放した。」

　日本側の史料は、鳥取藩で拘束していた安龍福をどのように処遇したか、そして米子—鳥取—長崎のルートで送り返したことが中心になっている。これに対して韓国側の史料は、安龍福の備辺司での供述にもとづいている。安龍福の足跡も、隠岐—伯耆藩—江戸幕府—長崎—対馬島となっており、日本側の記録と大きく異なっている。

　問題になるところは、第1に、隠岐で島主に鬱陵島が朝鮮の領土であると主張し、自分を拉致連行したのは不当であると抗議したかどうかについてである。その取調内容はわからないが、船頭の口上書では「御番所より唐人ニ酒一樽被遣候」と記してあることを、どのように考えるかが問題として残る。本人の意向に反して連行してきたことに対する陳謝の意味が込められていたのであろうか。

　第2は、隠岐国は幕府直轄の天領であり、大谷船が属する伯耆国とは関係がない。したがって、隠岐の役人が安龍福を鳥取藩に引渡したのではないのである。隠岐から米子に連行していったのは、大谷船の船頭が竹島渡海事業が朝鮮人によって妨害されている実情を訴え出るためで、安龍福らはそのための証人であった。

　第3に、米子での拘留は大谷邸内であり、鳥取藩はこれに足軽2人を警固役とした。取り調べは鳥取藩家老の荒尾大和と伯父の荒尾修理が担当した。安龍

福が竹島すなわち鬱陵島が朝鮮の領土であると主張したかどうかは確認できないが、言及した可能性についてまで否定することはできない。調書として鳥取の藩庁、さらには江戸の幕府に送られた「唐人ノ口書」、すなわち安龍福の供述がある。その内容はわからないが、「唐人ノ口書」が幕府に送られたことにより、幕府の竹島領有権についての認識が明確になり、朝鮮政府に対する朝鮮人の竹島渡海禁止の申し入れになったのであるから、何らかの主張が行われたものとみなければなるまい。

　もちろん、安龍福が述べているように、鳥取から江戸に送られ、幕府で審問した上で、鳥取藩主が鬱陵島は朝鮮領であるとする書契を安龍福に与えたなどというのは、すべて安龍福の作り話である。

　第4は、長崎から対馬藩に引渡されて以降は、安龍福に対する処遇が一変して罪人扱いになったことについてである。『朝鮮王朝実録』は、「伯耆州所給銀貨及文書馬島人劫奪」と記し、鳥取藩主からもらった銀貨も書契も対馬藩で没収されたというが、これは事実ではない。

　隠岐そして米子と鳥取で受けた対応は、たしかに厚遇というべきであろう。これに対して対馬藩の場合は、幕府の意向を受けて竹島への朝鮮人の渡海禁止を申し入れることになっている以上、安龍福らは越境侵犯の罪人として処遇されることになるのであった。

4　元禄9年の安龍福

1694（元禄7）年の竹島渡海は、荒天のために途中から引返している。

　同年11月、来春の渡海準備のため、村川、大谷両人は鳥取藩に例年通り資金の貸与を願い出た。併せて、竹島で朝鮮人に出会った時にはどのように対処したらよいかを伺い出た。これに対する鳥取藩の回答は、かつてないきびしいものであった。すなわち、「費用借用の儀度々なるを以て、之を許可せず、渡海の事は商売の勝手たる可く、朝鮮人在島の節の処置は差図に及び難し」というものである。

　あたかも、「竹島一件」と呼ばれる日朝両国間での外交交渉がはじまって1年を経過した時期である。朝鮮側は、それまでの「弊境之蔚陵島」と「貴界竹

島」といって別の島であるような表現をとっていた妥協説を改めて、「倭人所謂竹島、即我国鬱陵島」とする主張を述べて、日本側の譲歩を迫っていた。そうした情勢を反映して、鳥取藩においても竹島渡海事業の見直しがはじめられていたといえなくもない。そして1695（元禄8）年末には、鬱陵島は朝鮮領土であることを日本側も確認することで、「竹島一件」の結着を図る方向性がつくられ、1696年1月の幕府による竹島渡海の禁止令となる。

　隠岐に安龍福ら11人が着岸するのは、1696年の5月18日であった。すでに1月に幕府の渡海禁止令が出ているので、日本人の竹島渡海者はいなかったはずである。しかし安龍福が帰国後に備辺司で供述した記録—『朝鮮王朝実録』粛宗22年9月戊寅條には、全くちがった状況が記されているのである。慎鏞廈の著書から引用することにしたい。

　　「鬱陵島には、すでに日本の船がたくさん停泊していた。そこで安龍福が彼らに怒鳴りつけた。〝鬱陵島はもともとわれわれの島であるのに、日本人がなぜ国境を越えて入ってくるのか。〟

　　日本人がこう答えた。〝われわれはもともと松島（于山島、独島）に住む者だが、たまたま魚を追ってここに来たのであって、すぐ帰るつもりだ。〟

　　安龍福はこれに対して、〝松島は于山島で、やはりわれわれの島だ。どうして松島に住んでいるのか。〟と言い返した。

　　そして次の日、于山島に行ってみると、昨日の漁夫たちが釜で魚を煮ていたので、棒切れで追っ払ったところ、皆船に乗って日本へ帰って行った。

　　安龍福らは彼らを追って日本の隠岐島に上陸した。隠岐島主が安龍福に渡航理由を尋ねると、彼は大声で怒鳴った。〝何年か前、私が日本に来た時、鬱陵島、于山島などの島は朝鮮の領土に決まり、將軍の書状まで頂いたのに、日本は分別もなくわが領土を踏みにじるのか。〟

　　これに対し、隠岐島主は彼の抗議の内容を伯耆藩主に必ず伝えると約束した。しかしいくら待っても何の消息もなかった。安龍福はこれに憤慨し、船で伯耆に向かった。」

　鬱陵島で日本人に出会ったという話は、安龍福の作り話であって事実ではないことはすでに指摘した。その上で隠岐にやって来て、鬱陵島と子山島が朝鮮の領土であると主張したかどうか。村上家文書の「覚書」についてみよう。

　安龍福は、取り調べの在番役人に対して、「朝鮮八道之図」を差し出した。そこで竹島と松島については次のように述べている。

　　「安龍福が申すには、竹島は竹島と申し候、朝鮮国江原道東莱府の内に鬱陵島と申す島があり、是を竹の島と申す由、則ち八道之図にこれを記して所持仕り候」
　　「松島は右道の内、子山と申す島御座候、是を松島と申す由、是も八道之図に記し申し候」

　安龍福は、尋ねられていないにもかかわらず、竹島の鬱陵島、松島の子山島について述べているのである。しかも両島ともに朝鮮国の江原道東莱府に属しており、八道之図にも記してある通りという。八道之図なるものは持参しているといっていたが、村上家文書のなかには見られない。

　朝鮮八道を列挙した書面では、江原道のところで竹島と松島が記してある。また「此道ノ中ニ竹島松島有之」とあるが、他の道の島については記していないことからして、竹島と松島を朝鮮の領土として主張するために特別に作ってきたものと考えられる。

　竹島と松島の位置関係については、同じ「覚書」のなかで次のように記してある。

　　「当子三月十八日、朝鮮国朝食後に出船、竹島へは夕方着、夕飯を食べ申し候由」
　　「五月十五日竹島出船、同日松島着、同十六日松島を出て、十八日朝隠岐島の内西村の磯へ着」
　　「竹島と朝鮮の間三十里、竹島と松島の間五十里これあり申し候」

　韓国の蔚珍と鬱陵島の間は140キロ、鬱陵島と現竹島（松島、子山島、独島）

は92キロとされている。したがってここでいっているように、朝鮮本土と竹島の間が30里で、竹島と松島の間が50里というのは正確ではない。また、本土で朝食後に出発すると、鬱陵島には夕方に着くというのも、里数に合せていったものと思われる。ともあれ、こうした表現は、鬱陵島は朝鮮に近いこと、したがって朝鮮の領土であることをいいたいための配慮から出たものと思われる。

また時間距離では、5月15日に竹島を出発すると、同日中に松島に着く、16日に松島を出ると、18日の朝に隠岐に着いたといっているのは実態に合っている。1667（寛文7）年の斉藤豊仙による『隠州視聴合紀』でも、隠岐の北西方向に1泊2日で松島へ、さらに1日行くと竹島に到着すると記してある。

以上みてきたように、鬱陵島の竹島、子山島の松島についての位置関係の認識もたしかであり、両島はともに朝鮮国江原道東萊府に属する島であることを「朝鮮八道之図」を使って説明したこと、それを日本側の隠岐国在番役人が記録に書き留めたことなどが、明らかになったのが村上家文書の「元禄九丙午年朝鮮舟着岸一巻之覚書」である。

5 隠岐の安龍福

隠岐にやって来た安龍福が、鬱陵島の竹島、子山島の松島がともに朝鮮の領土であることを明示し、日本側の役人に記録させたことは、領有権問題をめぐる安龍福の役割を決定づける意味をもつ。日本側の記録のなかでは、村上家文書の「覚書」だけがそのことを記しており、鳥取藩の関係文書では見ることはできないのである。したがって、安龍福に子山島（独島）が朝鮮の領土であると日本側に主張した事実を確認できるものは、『朝鮮王朝実録』などの韓国側史料ではなく、隠岐での言動を記録したこの「覚書」というべきである。

なお、この「覚書」には、安龍福という人物を知るために重要と思われるいくつかの手がかりがある。

第1は、取り調べのなかで「癸酉十一月、日本にて下され候物共、書付の帳一冊出し申候、則写之申候」とある文言で、癸酉の年は元禄6年で、竹島から米子に連行された時のことである。

前述したように、鳥取藩でもらったという書契も銀貨も、帰国の時に対馬藩

で没収されたと、その後の備辺司で供述していたにもかかわらず、隠岐では日本でもらった物や書付をもってきたといっているのである。しかもその書付は、在番役人が写し取ったと述べているが、残念ながら現存していない。

　第2には、元禄9年に来日する直前のこととして、鬱陵島では日本人を怒鳴って追い払い、子山島では「松島即子山島、此亦我国地」といったとされているが、それが事実でないことは前述した通りである。

　しかし、竹島と松島が朝鮮の領土であるとする「八道之図」を用意して来日してきたことは明らかである。隠岐島主に抗議したかどうかは別にして、「伯耆守様江訴訟有之候て」隠岐に立ち寄ったもので、在番役人は「伯州へ訴訟のわけ書き出し候様に」と、安龍福に訴訟内容を詳細に書くことを求めている。これに対しての回答は、「書き出すには及ばず、伯州へ参り委細申し上ぐべき由」ということであった。だから隠岐の役所としては、抗議内容を鳥取藩に伝達することはできず、訴訟のために伯耆へ行くことだけしか連絡できなかったと思われる。

　第3に、6月4日に伯耆に行った安龍福は、船首に「朝鬱両島監税將臣安同知騎」と墨書した旗をかかげて青谷に着き、専念寺で鳥取藩から来意を尋ねられる。この時、安龍福は青帖裏の官服を着て、黒布の冠をかぶり、皮靴をはき、鳥取藩が用意したカゴに乗っていたと備辺司で供述しているが、隠岐で船内の道具を調べた前述の記録のなかには、官服や皮靴はもっていなかったのである。また、鳥取藩がカゴと馬を提供したのは鳥取の城下入りの時で、安龍福はそれを青谷でのことと誤認している。

　第4に、鳥取藩では外交使節として迎えられ、青谷から賀露を経て城下に入り、町会所を宿所とした。当然に藩の重臣と対談したと思われるが、それを安龍福は藩主に対座して鬱陵島への伯耆船の渡海について抗議したといっているが、そうではない。ただし、李仁成に書かせた訴文を鳥取藩に提出し、鳥取藩から江戸の藩邸に送り、そして幕府に届出た可能性についてまで全面否定することはできないと思う。

　それというのも、『朝鮮王朝実録』粛宗23年2月乙未條には、1697（元禄10）年2月に、対馬藩主が朝鮮の東萊府使に行った質問のなかで、「去秋、貴国人

呈單ノ事アリ、朝令ニ出ヅルカト」と尋ねたのに対して、東萊府使は「漂風ノ愚民ニ至リテハ、設ヒ作為スル所アルモ、朝家ノ知ル所ニ非ズ」と答えたことを記しているし、さらに『朝鮮通交大紀』が記す翌年3月の文書では、「呈書の事に至りては、誠に其の妄作の罪あり」とするのであった。それは、安龍福が日本で文書を提出したことを日朝両国がともに認めるものであり、そして文書を提出したとすれば鳥取藩に滞在中でということになる。

　第5に、隠岐に来た安龍福は、鬱陵島や子山島で渡海した日本人を怒鳴って追い払った男のイメージとは異なって、極めて友好的に振舞っており、これに隠岐の人たちも、できるだけの配慮をして友好的に対応していたことがわかるのである。

　在番役人の取り調べが終った時、安龍福は「心入れ」と称して、干鮑5包を在番役人へ、1包を大久村庄屋に贈ろうとした。これは受け取らず返却されたが、贈りものをしようとしたのは、みやげのつもりであったのか、世話になる御礼の意味が込められていたとみるべきであろうか。

　次いで朝鮮人たちは、船にもってきた米がなくなり、夕飯を食べていないと申し出る。大久村庄屋が船中を調べて、叺に3合の米しか残っていないことを見て可愛想に思い、凶年で米が少なかったにもかかわらず、村内から米をかき集めて4升5合を、さらに西郷の役所が届けてきた1斗2升3合の米を提供した。そのさい安龍福が、朝鮮では漂着船は救助して振舞っており、飯米がなくなったからには救助するのが当然であると述べたのに対して、大久村庄屋は、漂着したのであれば救助するが、伯耆州に訴願するために来たからには、飯米の用意はできているはずだといって、一度は申し出を断った上で米を与えているのである。

　また、毎日西風が強く、ゆれる船中では物書きができないので上陸させてほしいという申し出に対しては、海に近い百姓家を提供することにして、22日から安龍福ら4人が入居して訴訟のための下書をまとめたという。

　以上のようなエピソードは、安龍福の言動を考える場合に参考になるはずである。

　本稿で使用した村上家文書の「元禄九丙午年朝鮮舟着岸一巻之覚書」は、松

江市樋野俊晴氏解読によるものである。記して同氏のご芳情に謝意を表したい。